AmericanHeritage®

AMERICAN VOICES

CIVIL WAR AND RECONSTRUCTION

David C. King

WILEY

John Wiley & Sons, Inc.

CONTENTS

Introduction to the **AmericanHeritage**® American Voices Series

For more than four hundred years of our nation's history, Americans have left a long paper trail of diaries, letters, journals, and other personal writings. Throughout this amazingly vast collection, we can often find intriguing information about the events that make up that history. A diary entry, for example, can help us feel we are on the scene, as in this army officer's entry on the eve of a critical Revolutionary War battle: "It is fearfully cold, and a storm setting in. The wind is northeast and beats in the faces of the men. It will be a terrible night for the soldiers who have no shoes."

These firsthand accounts can also present us with surprises. In 1836, for instance, Narcissa Whitman was warned that hardship and possibly death awaited her on the rugged Oregon Trail. But from the trail she wrote: "Our manner of living is preferable to any in the States [the East]. I never was so happy and content before. Neither have I enjoyed such health." And personal writings can also take us inside the minds of people caught up in events, as in the case of Clara Barton, who became famous as a battlefield nurse in the Civil War but first had to wrestle with doubts about whether it was proper for a woman to tend wounded soldiers. "I struggled long and hard," she wrote, "with the appalling fact that I was only a woman . . . [but] thundering in my ear were the groans of suffering men dying like dogs [to save the society] that had protected and educated me."

Intriguing fragments like these make up our nation's history. Journals, letters, diaries, and other firsthand accounts are called primary sources. In addition to letters and journals, other voices from the past emerge from newspapers, books, and magazines, from poems and songs, from advertisements, pamphlets, and government documents. Added to the written records are "visual documents" such as sketches, diagrams, patent designs, maps, paintings, engravings, and photographs.

Historians have the fascinating work of sifting through these fragments, searching for the ones that will add a special touch to their reconstruction of the past. But historians are not the only ones who can appreciate these details. America's huge storehouse of primary materials offers a great opportunity to make history more interesting, exciting, and meaningful to everyone. History textbooks are useful for providing the bare bones of history, but firsthand accounts add the muscle and sinew, fleshing out the story with the experiences of real men and women. Primary sources also let you come to your own conclusions about what happened in the past, and they help you make connections between the past and the present.

In creating this series, we've looked for selections that draw out the drama, excitement, tragedy, and humor that have characterized the American experience. The cast of characters comes from a variety of backgrounds and time periods, but they all have authentic American voices, and they have all contributed to our nation's story. We have kept most of the selections short in order to include as many different voices and viewpoints as possible.

The language of primary sources can be difficult. For this series, we have modernized some of the spelling and grammar so that the texts are easier to understand, while being careful to maintain the meaning and tone of the original. We have also provided vocabulary and background information in the margins to help you understand the texts. For the most part, however, we have let the American voices speak for themselves. We hope that what they have to say will interest you, sometimes surprise you, and even inspire you to learn more about America's history.

Introduction to
Civil War and Reconstruction

Throughout the year 1861, in towns and cities throughout America, bands played and crowds cheered as young men in dashing uniforms marched off to war. The unusual thing about these scenes was that the eager young men were about to wage war not against some foreign invader, but against their fellow Americans, even members of their own families.

The central issue of the Civil War (1861–1865) was slavery, especially the question of extending slavery into the new territories and states being formed in the West. The issue so deeply divided the nation that eleven Southern states were determined to leave the Union of States, while the remaining states were just as determined to hold the Union together. But for the people in the crowds and the men marching, their passion had little to do with slavery. Instead, Southerners felt they were fighting for their independence and their way of life. Northerners fought for freedom and to put down a rebellion that threatened the very existence of the Union.

The Civil War was the bloodiest war in our history, claiming more lives than all of America's other wars combined. It was a conflict filled with the heroic and the tragic—a titanic struggle of huge armies locked in combat—but contained within it were individual stories that were dramatic, often brutal, sometimes beautiful, and occasionally comical.

The best way to find out what this war was like is to hear from the people who lived it. In this book you'll find a sampling of the nation's tremendous storehouse of letters, diaries, journals, songs, newspaper articles, memoirs, speeches, and novels from this period. You'll hear from three great U.S. senators as they attempt to reach one more compromise on the slavery issue. You'll be inside Fort Sumter with Captain Abner Doubleday as the first cannon shots of the war crash into the walls. And you'll learn about important battles from several points, including both Union and Confederate soldiers, the men in the front lines, as well as high-ranking officers, journalists, and civilians who found themselves in the path of the conflicts.

Women played a significant role throughout the war. Southerner Kate Cummings and Northerner Louisa May Alcott were among the first women to work as nurses, for example, while others, like Rose O'Neal Greenhow, were among a number of women who were successful as spies.

Today, as the events of the Civil War years drift farther into the past, people still find this period of our history haunting and fascinating. New books continue to emerge, examining every aspect of the war again and again. More than sixty thousand books have been published about this conflict—more than forty books for each day of the war. In many ways, however, the most exciting and rewarding accounts are those written by the men, women, and young people who were caught up in the events.

PART I

NORTH AND SOUTH DRIFT APART

From 1800 to 1850 the United States was growing rapidly and becoming increasingly prosperous. At the start of the century, people in both the North and the South assumed that the practice of slavery would soon disappear. It was already ending in the North, where slave labor was not practical for the small farms or the rapidly growing factories and mills. But in the South, Yankee Eli Whitney's invention of the cotton gin revolutionized the production of cotton as a cash crop. By the 1820s cotton plantations stretched from Georgia along the Gulf Coast to Texas. The cotton revolution happened just as textile mills in the North and in Western Europe needed more and more cotton to feed their high-speed looms, which were now mass-producing ready-made clothing and other textiles. As cotton production increased, so did the demand for slave labor. Between 1800 and 1860, the number of slaves doubled, then doubled again to nearly four million.

There were many thorny problems between the North and the South, but these were gradually worked out through the political process. After 1800, however, the issue of slavery drove a wedge deeper and deeper between the two regions. Compromise became more difficult as time passed. People in the South felt that their economy and their way of life depended on slavery; to defend it, they began arguing that there was nothing wrong with slavery and that, in fact, it served society well and was supported by the Bible. Northerners, in contrast, were becoming increasingly certain that their way of life was superior to the South's, and they developed the conviction that slavery must not be allowed in the West, where new territories were taking shape as America expanded westward.

Southerners were fearful that the North, with its much greater population, would soon control both houses of Congress and the presidency, giving them the power to force the South to end slavery. To maintain some measure of power, they counted on having equality in the U.S. Senate, where each state receives two senators. Consequently, whenever a free (nonslave) state applied for admission to the Union, leaders in Congress had to find a way to admit a slave state at the same time.

The readings in this part will provide evidence of how two different ways of living were emerging and how slavery was beginning to make those differences intolerable.

$\mathcal{T}$he Life of a Slave

Solomon Northrup was a free black who was kidnapped and sold into slavery. He labored on a Louisiana cotton plantation for twelve years before he finally regained his freedom. His story was written down by a friend and published as a book, *Twelve Years a Slave*.

DOCUMENTING THE AMERICAN SOUTH (http://docsouth.unc.edu), THE UNIVERSITY OF NORTH CAROLINA AT CHAPEL HILL LIBRARIES

Solomon Northrup, author of Twelve Years a Slave.

FROM
Solomon Northrup's
Twelve Years a Slave

1853

When a new hand is sent for the first time into the field, he is whipped up smartly and made for that day to pick as fast as he possibly can. At night his sack is weighed, so that his capability in cotton picking is known. He must bring in the same weight each night following. If it falls short, a greater or less number of lashes is the penalty.

An ordinary day's work is two hundred pounds. A slave who is accustomed to picking is punished, if he or she brings in less than that. . . .

The hands are required to be in the cotton field as soon as it is light in the morning. They are not permitted to be a moment idle until it is too dark to see. When the moon is full, they often labor till the middle of the night. . . . [After] the cotton is weighed . . . each one must attend to his respective chores. One feeds the mules, another the swine, another cuts the wood, and so forth.

Finally, at a late hour, they reach the quarters, sleepy and overcome with the long day's toil. Then a fire must be kindled in the cabin, the corn ground in the small hand-mill, and supper, and dinner for the next day in the field, prepared. All that is allowed them is corn and bacon, which is given out every Sunday morning. Each one receives, as his weekly allowance, three and a half pounds of bacon, and corn enough to make a **peck** of meal. That is all—no tea, coffee, sugar. Except for a very scanty sprinkling now and then, they have no salt.

peck: A unit of measurement equal to about eight quarts.

Slavery: Voices in Opposition

Most Northerners thought of slavery as a Southern problem and thought little about it. In the 1830s, however, a very vocal minority of Northerners began to speak out against slavery, arguing that it was against God's law. Some whites and blacks joined together to form the American Anti-Slavery Society. They used books, newspapers, and public rallies to denounce the hated institution. Their meetings, which often included African American speakers, aroused angry opposition from white audiences. Speakers were sometimes pelted with eggs or tomatoes; others were jailed or run out of town.

Oberlin, Ohio, became one of the centers of this *abolitionist* (in favor of outlawing, or abolishing slavery) sentiment. One of the most famous speakers and writers was the Reverend Theodore Weld. In the following selection, Weld lashes out at "the evils of slavery," focusing on the brutality of the most vicious slave masters.

FROM

Theodore Weld's American Slavery As It Is

1839

We will prove that slaves in the United States are treated with barbarous inhumanity; that they are overworked, underfed, wretchedly clad and lodged, and have insufficient sleep; that they are often made to wear around their necks iron collars armed with prongs, to drag heavy chains and weights at their feet while working in the field, and to wear yokes, and bells, and iron horns; that they are often kept confined in the stocks day and night for weeks together; made to wear gags in their mouths for hours or days, have some of their teeth torn out or broken off, that they may be easily detected when they run away; that they are frequently flogged with terrible severity, have red pepper rubbed into their lacerated flesh, and hot brine, spirits of turpentine, etc. poured over the gashes to increase the torture; that they are often stripped naked, their backs and limbs cut with knives, bruised and mangled by scores and hundreds of blows with the paddle . . . that they are often hunted with blood hounds and shot down like beasts, or torn in pieces by dogs. . . . All these things, and more, and worse, we shall *prove*. Reader, we know whereof we affirm, we have weighed it well; *more and worse* we will prove. Mark these words and read on; we will establish all these facts by the testimony of scores and hundreds of eye witnesses, by the testimony of *slaveholders* in all parts of the slave states, by slaveholding members of Congress and state legislatures. . . . We shall show, not merely that such deeds are committed, but that they are frequent; not done in corners, but before the sun; not in one of the slave states, but in all of them.

A Northern Mill Worker's Thoughts

One of the great differences between Northern and Southern life was the emergence of the factory system of production in the North. The mills built along New England's swift rivers and streams used water power to run machines that produced massive amounts of manufactured goods. The mills and factories provided cheap, ready-made clothing, tools, furniture, and housewares for families in all parts of the country. To run the looms and other machines, mill owners hired girls and young women from farm families, offering wages and a structured dormitory life. By the 1850s new immigrants from Europe began to fill the ever-increasing need for workers.

For many young women, life as a mill worker was an interesting change from life on the farm. Others found that the long hours and air polluted by clouds of lint and dust weakened their health. In one mill magazine, called the *Lowell Offering,* some of these young women expressed their thoughts and feelings. In the following selection, Elizabeth Turner reflects on the positive and negative aspects of being a "factory girl."

The Industrial Revolution

The use of machinery to produce goods and perform other work began transforming American life with the first New England mills and factories in the early 1800s. This great change is called the *Industrial Revolution*. By 1860, the Northern states had more than 74,000 mills; that was nearly 80 percent of the country's total.

Working conditions grew worse after the mid-1840s when owners began hiring managers to run the mills and factories. The owners gave up day-to-day control, and the managers were expected to reduce costs and increase profits. Workers who complained about longer hours or lower wages were fired. One manager said, "I regard my work-people just as I regard my machinery. . . . When my machines get old and useless, I reject them and get new, and these workers are part of my machinery."

FROM

The Lowell Offering

C. 1843

Evening is the time for thought and reflection. All is lovely outside, and why am I not happy? I cannot be, for a feeling of sadness comes stealing over me. I am far, far from that loved spot, where I spent the evenings of childhood years. I am here, among strangers—a factory girl—yes, *factory girl;* a name that is thought so degrading by many. . . .

But here I am. I toil day after day in the noisy mill. When the bell calls I must go. Must I always stay here, and spend my days within these walls, with this constant noise my only music?

I am sometimes asked, "When are you going home?" *Home,* that name ever dear to me. But they would not often ask me, if they only knew what sadness it creates to say, *"I have no home."* . . .

I will once more visit the home of my childhood. I will cast one long lingering look at the grave of my parents and brothers, and bid farewell to the spot. I have many friends who would not see me in want. I have uncles, aunts, and cousins, who have kindly asked me to share their homes. But I have a little pride yet. I will not be dependent upon friends while I have health and ability to earn bread for myself.

I will not always allow this sadness. I will wear a cheerful face, and make myself happy by contentment. I will earn all I can, and lay by something against a stormy day. I will do all the good I can, and make those around me happy as far as lies in my power. . . . I will spend my leisure hours in reading good books, and trying to acquire what useful knowledge I can. . . . I will try to live in reference to judgment day, and ever hope to meet my parents in a land of bliss.

"The Morning Bell," an engraving by Winslow Homer.

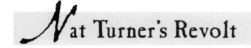

Nat Turner's Revolt

Because slaves outnumbered whites in many parts of the South, there was a constant anxiety that slaves might try to revolt. To guard against this, the slave states passed strict "black codes" to control the movements of slaves and free blacks. These codes, or laws, differed from state to state, but all prevented slaves—and often free blacks—from gathering in groups or being out at night without a pass. Violators of the codes were severely punished, and any attempt at an uprising was forcefully crushed.

Slaves who tried to fight their way to freedom had no real chance of success. But a few still tried. In 1822 a planned uprising in Charleston, South Carolina, was stopped by an informer. The leader, a free black named Denmark Vesey, and thirty-five slaves were hanged. In 1831 the most famous revolt took place when a slave named Nat Turner led his followers on a two-day killing spree in Virginia. With about eighty slaves and a few free blacks, "General" Turner's band murdered fifty-seven whites, mostly women and children. The state militia struck back, killing nearly one hundred blacks and capturing others, including Turner.

The following two news articles give very different reactions to the event. The first is from a Richmond newspaper's on-the-scene report; the second is from the leading abolitionist newspaper, the *Liberator*.

FROM

The Richmond Enquirer

"24TH AUGUST, 1831, 3 O'CLOCK"

A fanatic preacher by the name of Nat Turner (Gen. Nat Turner) who had been taught to read and write, and permitted to go about preaching in the country, was the bottom of this infernal brigandage. He was artful, impudent, and vindictive. . . . He was the slave of Mr. Travis. Turner . . . and another young fellow, by the name of Moore, [put together] a following mounted to the number of 40 or 50; and with knives and axes—knocking on the head, or cutting the throats of their victims. . . . But as they went from house to house, they drank **ardent** spirits—and it is supposed, that in consequence of their being intoxicated, or from mere fatigue, they paused in their murderous career about 12 o'clock on Monday.

A fact or two before we continue our narrative. These wretches are now estimated to have committed *sixty-one murders!* Not a white person escaped at all the houses they visited except two. . . .

The militia of Southampton had been most active in ferreting out the fugitives from their hiding places. . . . Nat, the ringleader, who calls himself General, pretends to be a Baptist preacher—a great enthusiast—declares to his comrades that he is commissioned by Jesus Christ, and proceeds under his inspired directions . . . is among the number not yet taken. The story of his having been killed at the bridge . . . is ungrounded. It is believed he cannot escape.

Northern Abolitionists

In the North, the 1830s witnessed the first ambitious efforts to speak out publicly against slavery, and a small but vocal group formed the American Anti-Slavery Society. While the society gained some support through the 1830s and 1840s, the majority of northern whites remained indifferent and some were openly hostile to the abolitionists. During the same period, a few African Americans also struck back at the hated institution. Some tried to revolt; others, who had gained their freedom, joined the Anti-Slavery Society.

FROM

The Liberator

SEPTEMBER 3, 1831

What we have long predicted,—at the peril of being stigmatized as an alarmist . . . —has commenced its fulfillment. The first step in the earthquake, which is ultimately to shake down the fabric of oppression, leaving not one stone upon the other, has been made. The first drops of blood, which are but the prelude to a deluge from the gathering clouds, have fallen. . . .

Read the account of the insurrection in Virginia, and say whether our prophecy be not fulfilled. . . .

True, the rebellion is quelled. Those slaves who were not killed in combat have been secured, and the prison is crowded with victims destined for the gallows! . . . You have seen, it is to be feared, but the beginning of sorrows. All the blood which has been shed will be aquired at your hands. At your hands alone? No—but at the hands of the people of New-England and of all the free states. The crime of oppression is national. The South is only the agent in this guilty traffic. But, remember! the same causes are at work which must inevitably produce the same effects; and when the contest shall have again begun, it must be a war of extermination. . . .

For ourselves, we are horror-struck at the late tidings. We have exerted our utmost efforts to avert the calamity. We have warned our countrymen of the danger of persisting in their unrighteous conduct. . . . How have we been received? We have been threatened, vilified and imprisoned. . . . If we have been hitherto urgent, and bold, and **denunciatory** in our efforts—hereafter we shall grow vehement and active with the increase of danger. We shall cry, in trumpet tones, night and day—Wo to this guilty land, unless she speedily repents of her evil doings!

The *Liberator*

The *Liberator* newspaper was founded in January 1831 by William Lloyd Garrison, one of the organizers of the American Anti-Slavery Society. It quickly became the most outspoken anti-slavery publication. Garrison wrote in the first issue, "I will not excuse—I will not retreat a single inch—AND I WILL BE HEARD!" Nat Turner's revolt took place just eight months after the first issue.

---

denunciatory: accusatory

The Amistad Affair

In 1840 a slave ship headed for Havana, Cuba, was taken over by the slaves, captives from the Mendi kingdom of Africa. The mutineers killed the captain, but, when trying to sail back to Africa, they lost their way and were picked up by the U.S. Revenue Cutter Service off Long Island. American authorities imprisoned them and they were put on trial for creating a slave uprising. When the case reached the U.S. Supreme Court in 1841, former president John Quincy Adams defended the captives, stating that "there is in my estimation no higher object upon earth . . . than to occupy that position [of defending the Africans]."

Adams, then in his mid-seventies, spoke brilliantly in a nine-hour closing argument that won the case and set the Africans free. In the process, he helped many Americans see slavery as a denial of basic American rights.

Joseph Cinque, a Mende from the Sierra Leone region of West Africa, led the Amistad revolt. After being freed by the U.S. Supreme Court, Cinque returned to his homeland only to find his village destroyed, his wife and children sold into slavery. He later worked for the American Missionary Association.

NATIONAL PORTRAIT GALLERY, SMITHSONIAN INSTITUTION/ART RESOURCE, N.Y.

Before the case was presented to the Supreme Court, the Africans chose one of their group, a boy named Kale, to write a letter to Adams to tell him of their cause. Although Kale was only eleven years old when captured, he learned English rapidly, as shown in the following excerpts from his letter.

FROM

Kale's Letter to John Quincy Adams

JANUARY 4, 1841

Dear friend Mr. Adams, you have children, you have friends, you love them, you feel very sorry if Mendi people come and take them all to Africa. We feel bad for our friends, and our friends all feel bad for us. Americans not take us in ship. We were on shore and Americans tell us slave ship catch us. They say we make you free. . . . If America give us free we glad, if they no give us free we sorry—we sorry for Mendi people, we sorry for America people great deal because God punish liars. We want you to tell court that Mendi people no want to go back to Havana, we no want to be killed. Dear friend, we want you to know how we feel. Mendi people think, think, think. . . . Mendi people have got souls. We think we know God punish us if we tell lie. We never tell lie; we speak the truth, what for Mendi people afraid? . . . Cook say he kill, he eat Mendi people—we afraid—we kill cook. Then captain kill one man with knife, and cut Mendi people plenty. We never kill captain if he no kill us. If Court ask who bring Mendi people to America, we bring ourselves. Ceci hold the rudder. All we want is make us free, not send us to Havana. Send us home. Give us Missionary. We tell Mendi people Americans spoke truth. We give them good tidings. We tell them there is one god. You must worship him. Make us free and we will bless you and all Mendi people will bless you, Dear friend Mr. Adams.

How Adams Won the Case

The basic argument John Quincy Adams presented to the Supreme Court was that the Mendi had been enslaved illegally because the international slave trade had been declared illegal some years earlier. Since the Mendi had been taken illegally, they had a right to fight for their freedom. (The two killings aboard the ship had taken place outside U.S. jurisdiction.) In agreeing with Adams, the justices made a point of stating that the ruling did not give slaves a right to revolt.

PART II

THE DEEPENING CRISIS

After 1850, relations between the North and South grew steadily worse, and many people began to feel that the country was helplessly drifting toward civil war. One reason for the deepening gloom was the issue of slavery in the new lands of the West. Southern leaders insisted that slavery could not be excluded from all the new territories and states. Northerners were increasingly determined to prevent any such extension.

Several attempts were made to find a compromise on this issue. When California applied for admission as a free state in 1850, a compromise was reached but it only postponed the conflict. Four years later, Illinois senator Stephen Douglas offered another solution, which he called "popular sovereignty," and this also failed to settle the matter. In 1857, the U.S. Supreme Court increased tensions by ruling in the *Dred Scott* case that slaves were property and their owners could take them anywhere.

The failure to resolve the issue of slavery in the West led a group of Northerners to form a new political party—the Republican party. In 1858, Republican Abraham Lincoln challenged Senator Douglas for his Senate seat. Lincoln lost the election, but his debates with Douglas made him a national figure and led to his nomination for the presidency in 1860.

Other events in this troubled decade convinced many Southerners that seceding from the Union of States might be the only way to preserve their way of life. People throughout the South were infuriated by the 1852 publication of Harriet Beecher Stowe's novel *Uncle Tom's Cabin*. They insisted that it gave a distorted view of slavery and of the South's way of life. And, in 1859, when abolitionist John Brown tried to start a slave rebellion by seizing the federal arsenal at Harpers Ferry, Virginia, many Southerners concluded that the abolitionists would try this again.

The readings in part II will show how these events carried America to the brink of war.

Key Events of the 1850s

1. The Compromise of 1850 and the Fugitive Slave Law. The South agreed to the admission of California as a free state, but the North was forced to accept a tough Fugitive Slave Law providing for the return of escaped slaves.

2. The publication of *Uncle Tom's Cabin,* 1852. Harriet Beecher Stowe's famous novel convinced many that slavery was evil and must be ended.

3. The Kansas-Nebraska Act, 1854. Congress passed a law for organizing the territories of Kansas and Nebraska, stating that the voters of Kansas would decide whether to allow slavery. This idea of "popular sovereignty" led both pro- and anti-slavery forces to rush settlers into Kansas. Violence erupted in what became known as "Bleeding Kansas."

4. The *Dred Scott* decision, 1857. This Supreme Court ruling had the effect of saying that slaves could be taken into all territories.

5. The Lincoln-Douglas debates, 1858. A series of debates between Abraham Lincoln and Senator Stephen Douglas focused the nation's attention on the issue of slavery in the territories and made Lincoln a national figure.

6. The raid on Harpers Ferry, 1859. John Brown's effort to start a slave uprising was a bloody failure, but it convinced Southerners that the North intended to use force to end slavery.

1850: The Last Compromise

The question of admitting California as a free state in exchange for a tough fugitive slave law dragged through the Senate for seven months. Three of the century's greatest senators were involved: Henry Clay of Kentucky, who proposed the compromise; John C. Calhoun of South Carolina, so close to death that he had to have a friend read his opposition to the plan; and Daniel Webster of Massachusetts, the great orator whose final speech led to approval of the compromise. These speeches are considered to be among the most dramatic and eloquent ever heard in the U.S. Congress. Selections from the three speeches are presented here.

FROM

Senator Henry Clay's Compromise Speech

FEBRUARY 5, 1850

California, with suitable boundaries, ought upon her application to be admitted as one of the States of the Union, without . . . any restriction in respect to the exclusion or introduction of slavery within those boundaries. . . . I call upon the free States . . . for the sake of peace, and in a spirit of forebearance to other members of the Union, to give up [their demand] that Congress exclude slavery from California. . . . Slavery is not likely to be introduced into any of those territories [of the west]. Is that not a fact? Is there a member of this body who doubts it? What has occurred within the last three months? In California, more than in any other portion of the territories, was it most probable . . . that slavery would be introduced; yet, within the last three months, slavery has been excluded by the vote—the unanimous vote—of the [California] Convention. . . .

Now, Mr. President [of the Senate], I think that the existing laws for the recovery of fugitive slaves . . . being often inadequate and ineffective, it is incumbent upon Congress . . . to make the laws more effective; and I will go with the furthest Senator from the South . . . to make **penal laws,** to impose the heaviest sanctions upon the recovery of fugitive slaves, and the restoration of them to their owners.

FROM

Senator John C. Calhoun's Answer for the South

MARCH 4, 1850

How can the Union be saved? There is but one way by which it can with any certainty; and that is, by a full and final settlement, on the principle of justice, of all the questions at issue between the two sections. The South asks for justice, simple justice, and less she ought not to take. She has no compromise to offer, but the Constitution; and no concession or surrender to make. She has already surrendered so much that she has little left to surrender. . . .

But can this be done? Yes, easily; not by the weaker party, for it can, of itself do nothing—not even protect itself—but by the stronger. The North has only to will it to accomplish it—to do justice by conceding to the South an equal right in the [western] territory, and to do her duty by causing the **stipulations** relative to fugitive slaves to be faithfully fulfilled, to cease the agitation of the slave question, and to provide for the insertion of a provision in the Constitution, by an amendment, which will restore to the South . . . the power she possessed of protecting herself, before the equilibrium between the sections was destroyed by the action of this Government. There will be no difficulty in devising such a provision—one that will protect the South, and which, at the same time, will improve and strengthen the government, instead of impairing and weakening it.

But will the North agree to this? It is for her to answer the question. . . . If you are unwilling we should part in peace. . . . If you remain silent, you will compel us to infer by your acts what you intend. In that case, California will become the test question. If you admit her, under all the difficulties that oppose her admission, you compel us to infer that you intend to exclude us from the whole of the . . . territories with the intention of destroying . . . the equilibrium between the two sections. We would be blind not to perceive in that case, that your real objects are power and **aggrandizement.**

aggrandizement: improving reputation or status.

The Role of the President

President Zachary Taylor opposed Clay's compromise and would not have signed the measure. But over the summer, Taylor became ill and died. Vice President Millard Fillmore became the new president and supported Clay's plan. As many people suspected, the compromise settled little; within a few months the slavery issue flared again over the Fugitive Slave Act.

FROM
Senator Daniel Webster's Speech for Compromise
MARCH 7, 1850

I wish to speak to-day, not as a Massachusetts man, nor as a northern man, but as an American, and a member of the Senate of the United States. . . . It is not to be denied that we live in the midst of strong agitations and are surrounded by very considerable dangers to our institutions and government. The imprisoned winds are let loose. The East, the North, and the stormy South combine to throw the whole sea into commotion, to toss its billows to the skies, and to disclose its profoundest depths. . . . I speak to-day for the preservation of the Union. "Hear me for my cause." I speak today out of a solicitous and anxious heart, for the restoration to the country of that quiet and that harmony which make the blessings of this Union so rich, and so dear to us all. . . .

Instead of speaking of the possibility or utility of secession, instead of dwelling in those caverns of darkness, instead of groping with those ideas so full of all that is horrid and horrible, let us come out into the light of day; let us enjoy the fresh air of Liberty and Union. . . . Never did there devolve on any generation of men higher trusts than now devolve upon us, for the preservation of this Constitution and the harmony and peace of all who are destined to live under it. Let us make our generation one of the strongest and brightest links in that golden chain which is destined, I fondly believe, to grapple the people of all the States to this Constitution for ages to come.

The Fugitive Slave Act

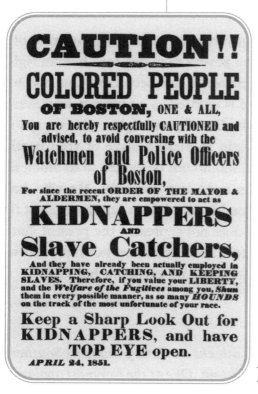

CAUTION!!
COLORED PEOPLE
OF BOSTON, ONE & ALL,
You are hereby respectfully CAUTIONED and advised, to avoid conversing with the
Watchmen and Police Officers of Boston,
For since the recent ORDER OF THE MAYOR & ALDERMEN, they are empowered to act as
KIDNAPPERS
AND
Slave Catchers,
And they have already been actually employed in KIDNAPPING, CATCHING, AND KEEPING SLAVES. Therefore, if you value your LIBERTY, and the *Welfare of the Fugitives* among you, Shun them in every possible manner, as so many *HOUNDS* on the track of the most unfortunate of your race.
Keep a Sharp Look Out for KIDNAPPERS, and have TOP EYE open.
APRIL 24, 1851.

Few acts could have outraged Northerners more than the Fugitive Slave Act, passed in 1850. Slave catchers from the South could now force Northern authorities to arrest anyone they said was an escaped slave. Even Northerners who cared little about ending slavery did not like the picture of alleged fugitive slaves being dragged in chains through the streets of their city. In the first of the following selections, Frederick Douglass, an escaped slave who became a leading abolitionist, expresses his outrage at the law. In the second selection, Charles E. Stevens describes the famous case of Anthony Burns, who, in 1854, was ordered by a Boston court to be returned to the Virginia plantation he had escaped from. Anti-slavery forces in Massachusetts could not bring themselves to use force to stop the procession and the crowd watched helplessly as Burns was taken to a ship.

An 1851 broadside warning African Americans in the North that Southern slave catchers and kidnappers were operating in Boston.

FROM

A Speech by Frederick Douglass

AUGUST 1852

The only way to make the Fugitive Slave Law a dead Letter is to make half a dozen or more dead kidnappers. A half dozen more dead kidnappers carried down South would cool the ardor of Southern gentlemen, and keep their rapacity in check. That is perfectly right as long as the colored man has no protection. The colored men's rights are less than those of a jackass. No man can take away a jackass without submitting the matter to twelve men [a jury] in any part of this country. A black man may be carried away without any reference to a jury. It is only necessary to claim him, and that some villain should swear to his identity. There is more protection there for a horse, for a donkey, or anything, rather than a colored—who is, therefore, justified in the eye of God in maintaining his right with his arm. . . .

Human government is for the protection of rights; and when human government destroys human rights, it ceases to be a government, and becomes a foul and blasting conspiracy; and is entitled to no respect whatever. . . . If you look over the list of your rights, you do not find among them any right to make a slave of your brother.

FROM

Charles E. Stevens's Eyewitness Account

JUNE 1854

At eleven o'clock, Court Square presented a spectacle that became indelibly engraved upon the memories of men. The people had been swept out of the square and stood crowded together on Court Street, presenting to the eye a solid rampart of living beings. At the eastern door of the Court House stood the cannon, loaded, with its mouth pointed full upon the compact mass. By its side stood the officer commanding the detachment of United States troops, gazing with steady composure in the same direction. It was the first time that the armed power of the United States had been arrayed against the people of Massachusetts. Men who witnessed the sight . . . were made painfully to recognize the fact, before unfelt, that they were the subjects of two governments. . . .

At length, about two o'clock, the column was formed in the square. First came a detachment of U.S. artillery, followed by a platoon of United States Marines. After these followed the armed civil posses of the marshal, [followed by] two platoons of Marines [which] brought up the rear. When this arrangement was completed, Burns, accompanied by an officer on each side with arms interlocked, was conducted from his prison through a passage lined with soldiers, and placed in the center of the armed posse. . . .

The route from the courthouse to the wharf had by this time become thronged with a countless multitude. It seemed as if the whole population of the city had been concentrated upon this narrow space. . . .

At different points along the route were displayed symbols significant of the prevailing sentiment. From a window opposite the Old State House was suspended a black coffin, upon which was the legend, "The Funeral of Liberty." At a point farther on toward the wharf, a venerable merchant had caused a rope to be stretched across State Street to an opposite point, and the American Flag, draped in mourning, to be suspended therefrom with the union down. . . .

The column now began to move. No music enlivened its march; the dull tramp of the soldiers on the rocky pavements and the groans and hisses of the bystanders were the only sounds. . . . In its progress, it went past the Old State House. . . . Just below, it passed over the ground where, in the massacre of 1770, fell Crispus Attucks, the first Negro martyr in the cause of American liberty.

The Underground Railroad

One of the most dramatic responses to the Fugitive Slave Act was the Underground Railroad. The "Railroad" was not an actual railroad nor was it physically underground, but instead it was a constantly shifting network of routes through the upper South and the North. Escaped slaves, usually guided by a "conductor," could find help and shelter along one of these routes until they reached safety, often in Canada, where they would be beyond the reach of the slave catchers.

The Underground Railroad seems to have started as early as the 1780s, but it became most active after passage of the Fugitive Slave Act. Historians estimate that roughly fifty thousand slaves made their way to freedom through this system.

The following three selections describe how the Underground Railroad worked: the first is by Levi Coffin of Ohio. (Coffin was a *Quaker*, a member of a religious sect based on a philosophy of the equality of all peoples and a belief in nonviolence.) Like many Quakers, he was a major organizer of the system. The second selection tells of Henry Brown's creative escape; and the third is about the work of Harriet Tubman, an escaped slave who went south again and again to help free an estimated three hundred slaves. Her story was written by William Still, the son of former slaves, who kept detailed records of underground activities in the Philadelphia area.

FROM

Levi Coffin's Recollections

C. 1850

The fugitives generally arrived at night, and were secreted among the friendly colored people or hidden in the upper room of our house. They came alone or in companies, and in a few instances had a white guide to direct them.

One company of twenty-eight that crossed the Ohio River at Lawrenceburg, Indiana—twenty miles below Cincinnati—had for conductor a white man whom they employed to assist them. . . . John Fairfield conducted the party to the Ohio River . . . [where] the entire party made their way to three large skiffs or **yawls,** and made their way slowly across the river. The boats were overloaded and sank so deep that the passage was made in much peril. . . . The entire party waded through mud and water and reached the shore safely, though all were wet and several lost their shoes.

They hastened along the bank toward Cincinnati, but it was now late at night and daylight appeared before they reached the city. Their plight was a most pitiable one. They were cold, hungry, and exhausted; those who had lost their shoes . . . suffered from bruised and lacerated feet, while to add to their discomfort a drizzling rain fell. They could not enter the city for their appearance would at once proclaim them to be fugitives. . . . John Fairfield hid them as well as he could, in ravines . . . and told them not to move until he returned.

He then went directly to John Hatfield . . . a deacon in the Zion Baptist Church and told his story . . . and Hatfield at once sent a merssenger to me. . . . I went at once. While dry clothes and a warm breakfast were furnished to John Fairfield, we anxiously discussed the situation of the twenty-eight fugitives who were lying hungry and shivering in the hills in sight of the city. . . .

I suggested that some one go to a certain German livery stable and hire two coaches, and that several colored men should go out in buggies and take the women and children from their hiding places, then that the coaches and buggies should form a procession as if going to a funeral, and march

A young former slave who was probably brought north on the Underground Railroad about 1855. The photo, found in a Pennsylvania home, is a rare form called an ambrotype, which was made in the camera with no negative plate, creating a one-of-a-kind photo.

yawl: boats equipped with oars as well as sails.

solemnly along the road leading to Cumminsville. . . . All the arrangements were carried out, and the party reached College Hill in safety, and were kindly received and cared for.

ᘐᖆ ᘐᖆ ᘐᖆ ᘐᖆ ᘐᖆ ᘐᖆ ᘐᖆ ᘐᖆ ᘐᖆ ᘐᖆ ᘐᖆ ᘐᖆ ᘐᖆ ᘐᖆ ᘐᖆ

FROM

Henry "Box" Brown's Account

C. 1852

Searching for a way to escape on a ship with the help of a friend, there darted into my mind these words, "Go and get a box, and put yourself in it. . . ." I then repaired to a carpenter, and induced him to make me a box two feet eight inches deep, two feet wide, and three feet long.

When the box was finished, I carried it, and placed it before my friend, who had promised to assist me. . . . I took my place in this narrow prison, with a mind full of uncertainty as to the result. . . . I laid me down in my darkened home of three feet by two, and like one about to be guillotined, resigned myself to my fate. . . .

I took with me a bladder filled with water to bathe my neck with, in case of too great heat; and with no access to the fresh air, excepting three small drill holes, I started my perilous cruise. . . . I was first carried to the express office, the box being placed on its end, so that I started with my head downwards. . . . I was put on board the steamboat and placed on my head! In this dreadful position, I remained . . . when I began to feel of my eyes and head, and found to my dismay, that my eyes were almost swollen out of their sockets, and the veins on my temple seemed ready to burst. [The box was finally placed right side up and Brown arrived safely in Philadelphia; there, a "stationmaster" for the Underground Railroad pulled him from his hiding place.]

FROM

William Still's Account of Harriet Tubman

C. 1870

Her success was wonderful. Time and again she made successful visits to Maryland on the Underground Railroad and would be absent for weeks at a time, running daily risks while making preparations for her safety, but she seemed wholly devoid of personal fear. . . .

While she thus manifested such utter personal indifference, she was much more watchful with regard to those she was piloting. Half of her time, she had the appearance of one asleep, and would actually sit down by the roadside and go fast asleep when on her errands of mercy through the South. Yet, she would not suffer one of her party to whimper once about "giving out and going back," however wearied they might be from hard travel day and night. . . .

After having once enlisted, "they had to go through or die." Of course Harriet was supreme, and her followers generally had full faith in her and would back up any word she might utter. So when she said to them that "a live runaway could do great harm by going back, but that a dead one could tell no secrets," she was sure to have obedience. . . . Her success . . . was attributable to her adventurous spirit and utter disregard of consequences. Her like it is probable was never known before or since.

During the Civil War, Harriet Tubman, already known as the "Moses of her people" for leading them to freedom, came to the aid of a Union regiment operating in the islands off South Carolina. She worked there as a cook, laundress, and nurse, except when she was needed to scout for an army unit or go behind Confederate lines as a spy.

Harriet Beecher Stowe and Uncle Tom's Cabin

Harriet Beecher Stowe, the daughter of a leading abolitionist minister, created her own powerful response to the Fugitive Slave Act. Her novel *Uncle Tom's Cabin* was published in 1852, and caused an immediate sensation. More than three hundred thousand copies were sold within the first year; more than seven million copies were eventually sold throughout the world. In 1852, George Aiken made it into a play, without Stowe's consent, and the play also enjoyed great success.

Stowe's story about the evils of plantation slavery helped convince many Northerners of the evils of the slave system. Southern newspaper editors expressed outrage, arguing that Stowe had never even seen a plantation and gave a distorted picture of slavery. Through the 1850s, the book and the stage play continued to harden Northern attitudes against slavery and to increase Southern defensiveness. Many readers in the North who knew little or nothing about slavery were transformed into abolitionists by this story.

Uncle Tom's Cabin, or, Life among the Lowly has never been considered great literature, but it is a very dramatic story, filled with unforgettable characters and tragic events. The plot centers around an elderly Christian slave, Uncle Tom, who dies at the hands of a cruel foreman, or overseer, named Simon Legree, when he tries to save a woman from being whipped. Tom refuses to surrender his belief in God, and he shows his kindness by helping a slave family escape on the Underground Railroad.

The first of the following selections is a brief scene from the novel in which the vicious overseer, Simon Legree, tries to force Uncle Tom into administering a beating. The second selection is from the last chapter, in which Stowe speaks directly to the reader to answer the question *Would African Americans be able to take care of themselves once they were free?*

Harriet Beecher Stowe, author of Uncle Tom's Cabin

Stowe and Lincoln

When Stowe was introduced to President Lincoln during the Civil War, it is reported that he said, "So this is the little lady who started this big war."

FROM

Uncle Tom's Cabin

1852

Slowly the weary, dispirited creatures, wound their way into the room, and, with crouching reluctance, presented their baskets to be weighed.

Legree noted on a slate, on the side of which was pasted a list of names, the amount.

Tom's basket was weighed and approved; and he looked, with an anxious glance, for the success of the woman he had befriended.

Tottering with weakness, she came forward, and delivered her basket. It was of full weight, as Legree well perceived; but, affecting anger, he said,

"What, you lazy beast! short again! stand aside, you'll catch it, pretty soon!"

The woman gave a groan of utter despair, and sat down on a board. . . .

"And now," said Legree, "come here, you Tom. You see, I told ye I didn't buy ye jest for the common work; I mean to promote ye, and make a driver of ye; and to-night ye may jest as well begin to get yer hand in. Now, ye jest take this yer gal and flog her; ye've seen enough on't to know how."

Contributions to Our Language

The term "Uncle Tom" came to be applied to any African American who tried to gain the favor of white Americans. This is a misuse of the term, however, since Uncle Tom preferred to lose his life rather than yield to a cruel white man.

"Simon Legree" is a label that has been used more accurately to describe someone who acts cruelly or viciously in a position of power or authority.

FROM

The Last Chapter of Uncle Tom's Cabin

1 8 5 2

The author gives the following statements of facts with regard to emancipated slaves now living in Cincinnati. They are given to show the capability of the race, even without any particular help and encouragement. . . .

B———. Furniture maker. Twenty years in the city. Worth ten thousand dollars, all the result of his own earnings. . . .

C———. Stolen from Africa. Sold in New Orleans. Been free fifteen years. Paid for himself six hundred dollars [for his freedom]. A farmer, owns several farms in Indiana. Probably worth fifteen or twenty thousand dollars, all earned by himself.

K———. Dealer in real estate. Worth thirty thousand dollars. About forty years old. Free six years. Paid eighteen hundred dollars for his family. Received a legacy from his master, which he has taken good care of and increased.

G———. Coal dealer. About thirty years old. Worth eighteen thousand dollars. Made all his money by his own efforts—much of it while a slave, hiring his time from his master and doing business for himself. A fine, gentlemanly fellow. . . .

The writer well remembers an aged colored woman. She was employed as a washerwoman in her father's family. The daughter of this woman married a slave. She was a remarkably active and capable young woman.

By her industry and thrift and self-denial, she raised nine hundred dollars for her husband's freedom. She paid, as she raised it, into the hands of his master. She yet lacked a hundred dollars for the full price for her husband when he died. She never recovered any of the money.

These are but a few facts to show the self-denial, energy, patience, and honesty that the slave has exhibited in a state of freedom.

Bleeding Kansas

In the late 1850s, politicians struggled to find some way to hold the Union of States together. Nothing worked. In 1854, Congress passed the Kansas-Nebraska Act, using the idea of "popular sovereignty—the brain-child of Illinois senator Stephen Douglas—which meant that the voters of new territories or states could decide for themselves whether to allow slavery. The result was "Bleeding Kansas"—five years of sporadic violence by both pro-slavers and Free Soilers that led to more than two hundred deaths.

In 1855, a year after the Kansas-Nebraska Act was passed, Kansas held its first territorial election. For months pro-slave men had been rushing into Kansas from neighboring Missouri. These "Border Ruffians," most of them well armed, were determined to create a pro-slavery government. A New England abolitionist group encouraged hundreds of anti-slavery people to head for Kansas so that they could outnumber the pro-slavery voters. These settlers became known as "Free Soilers."

When the election was held, fifteen hundred voters were registered, but more than six thousand votes were cast! So many Border Ruffians had crossed over that the pro-slavers easily won the election and approved a constitution making it a crime to question the legality of slavery. Anti-slave forces held a second election, in 1857, which their candidates won. The Free Soilers wrote a new constitution outlawing slavery in Kansas. After years of sporadic violence, Congress finally recognized the anti-slavery government and constitution. By 1860, the Census indicated that there were only two slaves in all of Kansas.

In the following selection, Julia Lovejoy, a Free Soiler and correspondent for several Northern newspapers, describes the aftermath of one of the encounters in the seesaw struggle for Kansas. The reading offers evidence of why the violence in Kansas came to be regarded as a preview of the Civil War.

FROM

Julia Lovejoy's Letter to a New Hampshire Newspaper

SEPTEMBER 5, 1856

Our hearts sicken at the atrocities perpetrated daily upon the innocent and unoffending.—Ossawattamie has been laid in ashes, every house burned, and four of our men killed.—The gallant Brown [not John Brown], while searching after his saddle, was shot dead in the street. Fifty Ossawattamie families shelterless, are now living in their wagons in the woods, endeavoring to escape these fiends in human form. . . . This was a beautiful town. . . . Jude Wakefield's house and four of his neighbors' were burnt night before last. The ruffians have burnt every Free State man's house in Leavenworth, pressed the men into their service, at the peril of their lives, driven the women and children, with just the clothers on their backs, into the boats and sent them down the river. Children with no parents to take care of them, were pushed into the boat and sent off too!

Our men have driven off their army twice this week. . . . At Black Jack the two armies were drawn up in line of battle, a ravine separating them, but after viewing our brave fellows, they concluded that running was the better part of valor, and took to their heels, and put spurs to their horses. . . .

The people of Westport have great cause for alarm, for the ghosts of murdered victims, we have no doubt, are haunting the place, and ere long their blood will be avenged!

Our men have gone over the river, to help the Delaware Indians today. The Ruffians are stealing their horses, and committing other depredations amongst them, burning one of their houses and an Indian boy with it—this will arouse their ire, and they are a powerful tribe. Now these fellows will find they have got somebody besides Yankees to fight!

Massacre at Pottawatomie Creek

In 1855, pro-slave forces in Kansas attacked the anti-slavery government located in the town of Lawrence. The mob burned, looted, wrecked printing presses, and killed a man. A revenge raid was led by a fiery abolitionist named John Brown of Connecticut. Brown's small band raided a settlement at Pottawatomie Creek, where they dragged five men and boys from their beds and shattered their skulls with a sword, killing them all. The brutal murders were only part of the bloody fighting in Kansas that eventually claimed more than two hundred lives.

The Dred Scott Decision

In 1846, a slave named Dred Scott sued in the courts for his freedom. The basic argument used by his lawyers was that his owner, a physician, had taken him to live for a time in Illinois, a free state, and then into a free territory. Because Scott had lived in free territory, they argued, he was legally a free man. The case slowly made its way through the lower courts. Then, early in 1857, the justices of the U.S. Supreme Court decided to use the case to settle the issue of slavery in the territories once and for all. Few Supreme Court decisions have aroused more controversy than the one handed down by Chief Justice Roger B. Taney in March 1857. In the selection from the Court's decision that follows, Taney argued first that the founders of the United States had never intended for Africans or their descendants to be part of the "people"; his second argument was that slaves were property and an owner could take his property wherever he pleased. Northerners, including many who were not abolitionists, were outraged by the Court's statement that blacks were inferior to whites and that slavery was a natural condition for blacks.

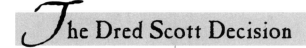

FROM

Chief Justice Roger B. Taney's Opinion in Dred Scott v. Sandford

MARCH 1857

In the opinion of the Court, the legislation and histories of the times, and the language used in the Declaration of Independence, show that neither the class of persons who had been imported as slaves nor their descendants, whether they had become free or not, were then acknowledged as a part of the people. . . .

They had for more than a century before been regarded as beings of an inferior order and altogether unfit to associate with the white race, either in social or political relations;

and so far inferior that they had no rights which the white man was bound to respect; and that the Negro might justly and lawfully be reduced to slavery for his benefit. . . .

It is the opinion of the Court that . . . Congress [cannot] prohibit a citizen from holding and owning property of this kind [that is, slaves] in the territory of the United States; and that neither Dred Scott himself, nor any of his family, were made free by being carried into [free] territory. . . . [In addition] Scott and his family, upon their return [from free territory] were not free, but were by the laws of Missouri, the property of the defendant; and the [federal courts] had no jurisdiction when by the laws of the state, the plaintiff was a slave and not a citizen.

Reaction to the Dred Scott Decision

While Southerners cheered the Court decision, saying that slave owners could now take their property wherever they pleased, most people in the North were horrified. The headline of the *New York Independent* announced: "The Decision of the Supreme Court Is the Moral Assassination of a Race and Cannot Be Obeyed." The decision also won support for the new Republican party because of its firm stand against extending slavery into the West.

The Lincoln-Douglas Debates

When the new Republican party nominated Abraham Lincoln to run against Stephen Douglas in the 1858 Senate election, few voters knew who Lincoln was. Lincoln had served a single term in Congress in 1846, but his opposition to America's war with Mexico cost him any chance of reelection.

The 1858 election campaign transformed the tall, awkward-looking attorney into a national figure. When Lincoln started his campaign, his audiences and newspapers were impressed by his arguments and his engaging speaking style, which was filled with humorous stories, often poking fun at himself or Senator Douglas. As the crowds grew larger, Lincoln gained confidence and, in July, challenged Senator Douglas to a series of seven debates. Audiences numbered almost twenty thousand and, even though the arguments were long (two hours or more) and complicated, people listened closely.

The key issue in the debates, of course, was the extension of slavery into the territories. Douglas defended his doctrine of "popular sovereignty"—letting the voters decide whether to allow slavery—while Lincoln probed for weaknesses in the doctrine. Lincoln, in turn, argued that the nation could not exist "half-slave and half-free," and Douglas attacked this idea by saying it would force the South to secede.

Lincoln did well in the popular vote, but senators were actually elected by the state legislature, and the Democrats still had firm control of Illinois. Douglas kept his Senate seat but Lincoln gained fame. The two men emerged as likely candidates of their respective parties for the presidency in 1860. The first of the following selections is a famous passage from Lincoln's "house divided" speech, and the second reading is Douglas's reply.

FROM

Lincoln's "House Divided" Speech

1858

A House divided against itself cannot stand. I believe this government cannot endure permanently half-slave and half-free. I do not expect the Union to be dissolved. I do not expect the house to fall—but I do expect it will cease to be divided. It will become all one thing, or all the other. Either the opponents of slavery will arrest the further spread of it, and place it where the public mind shall rest in the belief that it is in the course of ultimate extinction, or its advocates will push it forward till it shall become alike lawful in all the States—old as well as new, North as well as South.

FROM

Stephen Douglas's Response to Lincoln

1858

Mr. Lincoln tried to avoid the main issue by attacking the truth of my proposition, that our fathers made this government divided into free and slave states. Did they not thus make it? . . . They agreed to form a government uniting [the states] together, as they stood divided into free and slave States, and to guarantee forever to each State the right to do as it pleased on the slavery question. Having thus made the government, and conferred this right upon each State forever, I assert that this government can exist as they made it, divided into free and slave States. He says he looks forward to a time when slavery shall be abolished everywhere. I look forward to a time when each State shall be allowed to do as it pleases. . . . I care more for the great principle of self-government, the right of the people to rule, than I do for all the Negroes in Christendom.

John Brown's Raid on Harpers Ferry

On the rainy night of October 16, 1859, a band of twenty-one armed men—white and black—raided the U.S. arsenal at Harpers Ferry, Virginia. Their leader, the wild-eyed abolitionist John Brown, planned to use the arsenal weapons to arm the slaves, whom he thought would immediately join him in a great insurrection. But there was no uprising, and the raiders were quickly surrounded and trapped. Some were killed, and Brown and the others were captured, tried, and executed.

The following reading was typical of the often fragmented news reports that came over the telegraph wires during or immediately after any event; it will help you understand why Southerners feared that this raid was just the beginning of attempts to create a slave revolt. The event also led many Northerners to feel that war could no longer be avoided. The second selection is Brown's prediction of war, written as a note he handed a guard on his way to the gallows.

FROM

A Telegraphed News Dispatch from Baltimore

OCTOBER 17, 1859

To the Associated Press

A dispatch just received here from Frederick (Maryland), and dated this morning, states that an insurrection has broken out at Harper's Ferry, where an armed band of Abolitionists have full possession of the Government Arsenal. . . .

Another account, received by train, says the bridge across the Potomac was filled with insurgents, all armed. Every light in the town was extinguished, and the hotel closed. All the streets were in the possession of the mob, and every road and lane leading thereto barricaded and guarded. Men were seen in every quarter with muskets and bayonets, who arrested the citizens, and impressed them into service, including many negroes. . . . Some were of the opinion that the object was entirely plunder, and to rob the Government of the funds deposited on Saturday at the Pay-house. During the night, the mob made a demand on the Wager Hotel for provisions, and enforced the claim by a body of armed men. The citizens were in a terrible state of alarm, and the insurgents have threatened to burn the town.

John Brown's Prediction

DECEMBER 2, 1859

I John Brown am now quite *certain* that the crimes of this *guilty land will* never be purged *away;* but with Blood. I had as *I now think; vainly* flattered myself that without very much blood-shed; it might be done.

John Brown: Villain or Martyr?

Most people, North and South, were horrified by John Brown's raid. Throughout the South, troops were called out to be prepared for another uprising. In the North, most people condemned the use of violence. The most surprising response came from leading literary figures in the North who considered Brown a martyr—a sacrifice to the cause of freedom and justice. Here are some sample statements:

- Poet Henry Wadsworth Longfellow called it "the day of a new revolution, quite as much needed as the old one."

- Essayist and poet Ralph Waldo Emerson called Brown "a new saint, who will make the gallows glorious like the cross."

- Black poet Frances E. W. Harper declared, "Already from your prison has come a shout of triumph against the great sin of our country."

- Essayist Henry David Thoreau observed, "In teaching us how to die, [he has] at the same time taught us how to live."

A Currier & Ives lithograph of John Brown from Louis Ransom's sympathetic painting. The painting is based on a story of Brown meeting a slave and her child as he left the jail on the way to his execution.

The Election of 1860: Two Presidents

The presidential election of 1860 brought the North-South crisis to a decisive point. Southern leaders said they would not accept Lincoln as their president if elected because his Republican party was dedicated to ending slavery. Lincoln denied this. After his election in November 1860, it was a long time before his inauguration in March 1861. Throughout this period he tried to reassure the South that he would not interfere with slavery where it already existed.

Southern leaders refused to listen. Even before Lincoln's inauguration, seven Southern states (with four more soon to follow) had voted to secede from (or leave) the Union and form the Confederate States of America (C.S.A.). Jefferson Davis, who had been a senator from Mississippi, became the president of the C.S.A. America now had two governments and two presidents. In the following selections, two distinguished writers give their impressions of the two presidents. William Russell, a journalist for the *London Times,* described President Jefferson Davis in his diary; and Nathaniel Hawthorne, author of such books as *The Scarlet Letter* and *The House of the Seven Gables,* wrote his impressions of President Lincoln.

COURTESY NATIONAL ARCHIVES

Jefferson Davis, president of the Confederate States of America.

FROM

William Russell's Diary

1863

I had an opportunity of observing President [Jefferson Davis] very closely: He did not impress me as favorably as I had expected, though he is certainly a very different looking man from Mr. Lincoln. He is like a gentleman—has a slight light figure, little exceeding middle height, and holds himself erect and straight. He was dressed in a rustic suit of slate-colored stuff, with a black handkerchief round his neck; his manner is plain, and rather reserved. . . . Wonderful to relate, he does not chew [tobacco], and is neat and clean-looking, with hair trimmed and boots brushed. The expression of his face is anxious, he has a very haggard, careworn, and pain-drawn look, though no trace of anything but the utmost confidence and the greatest decision could be detected in his conversation. He asked me some general questions respecting the route I had taken in the States.

FROM

Nathaniel Hawthorne's "Sketches"

1862

By and by there was a little stir on the staircase and in the passageway, and in lounged a tall, loose-jointed figure . . . whom (as being about the homeliest man I ever saw, yet by no means repulsive or disagreeable) it was impossible not to recognize as Uncle Abe.

Unquestionably, Western man though he be, and Kentuckian by birth, President Lincoln is the essential representative of all Yankees. . . . There is no describing his lengthy awkwardness nor the uncouthness of his movements; and yet it seemed as if I had been in the habit of seeing him daily, and had shaken hands with him a thousand times in some village street. . . .

The whole physiognomy is as coarse a one as you would meet anywhere in the length and breadth of the States;

Varina Howell Davis

Born into the plantation aristocracy in Mississippi, Varina Howell was educated in Philadelphia. This Northern connection led to the wartime criticism that she was sympathetic to the Union cause, and, like Mary Todd Lincoln, she had several relatives in the uniform of the enemy, in her case, the Union. She was a vital support to her husband during the war and, when he was later imprisoned, she persuaded the federal authorities to let her share his imprisonment. When he was released in 1867, they lived quietly on a Mississippi plantation. After her husband's death in 1889, she wrote her own account of the role of Jefferson Davis in the Confederacy. She lived in New York City until her death in 1906 at the age of eighty.

but withal, it is redeemed, illuminated, softened, and brightened by a kindly though serious look out of his eyes, and an expression of homely sagacity, that seems weighted with rich results of village experience. A great deal of native sense; no bookish cultivation, no refinement; honest at heart, and thoroughly so. . . . On the whole, I like this sallow, queer, sagacious visage, with the homely human sympathies that warmed it; and for my small share in the matter, would as lief have Uncle Abe for a ruler as any man whom it would have been practicable to put in his place.

President Abraham Lincoln and his son Tad (Thomas), 1864.

Mary Todd Lincoln

Few of America's First Ladies have had such a difficult role to play as did Mary Todd Lincoln. There were many stories about her erratic behavior and arguments with her husband, but she seems to have been a steadying influence on him during the strain of the war years. When she tried to maintain some sort of White House social life, she was criticized for making light of the war; but when she took an interest in political matters, critics said she was meddling. Because she was from the South (Lexington, Kentucky), she was often accused of being sympathetic to the Confederacy, especially since her four brothers and three brothers-in-law served in the Confederate armies. She overcame these difficulties and the death of a son in the White House, but suffered from deep depressions after Lincoln's assassination. After a year in a mental hospital, she was declared sane and released to spend her remaining years with her sister. She died in 1882.

PART III

THE WAR BEGINS

As the nation drifted closer to war, some people were horrified at the idea of Americans killing each other. But many on both sides were thrilled by the prospect of military action, and they were confident their side would win after a short and glorious war.

On paper, all the facts favored the North. The states of the Union, for example, had a much larger population—22.5 million people; the South's population was only 9 million and nearly 4 million of that total were slaves. In addition, the North had an enormous advantage in industry, producing nine times as many manufactured goods, and the North had twenty-four times as many locomotives and thirty-three times as many weapons. The people of the North were sure that their military and industrial power would quickly crush the Confederacy.

People in the South had their own reasons for confidence. They would be fighting a defensive war, protecting their homes and families from the Yankee invaders. Lincoln's armed forces would have to try to conquer and occupy large areas of the South; when Northerners saw how impossible that task was, their morale would sag and they would grow weary of a winless war. Southerners also were proud of their military tradition. Most of the top officers in the U.S. Army were Southerners, trained at West Point or at Southern military schools. Many Southern young men had cavalry training and they would be going to war with their own horses. They thought of Northerners as farmers and immigrant laborers who knew nothing about war.

Americans had not fought a war since the war with Mexico (1846–1848), and that had been fought almost entirely on Mexican soil. Few could remember the previous conflict, the War of 1812, a half-century earlier. So the sight of troops marching, carrying banners and rifles with glistening bayonets, while bands played and crowds cheered, gave the idea of war a romantic aura. Few people were prepared for what was to come.

New York's Seventh Regiment marching down Broadway to join the Army of the Potomac.

*O*n the Eve of War

As soon as Lincoln was elected, South Carolina voted to secede and six other states quickly followed. Once they had formed the Confederacy, their troops began to take over federal forts and arsenals located in the South. The outgoing government of James Buchanan felt powerless to stop the takeover. In the spring of 1861, four more states joined the Confederacy, including Virginia.

During these months of uneasy peace, Northerners and Southerners expressed their feelings—some confident, others anxious. The following selections provide evidence of the war spirit in both the North and the South. The first reading is a letter from Boston; the second is from Nashville, Tennessee.

FROM

George Ticknor's Letter to an English Friend

APRIL 21, 1861

I never before knew what popular excitement can be. . . . Indeed, here at the North, at least, there never was anything like it. . . . The whole population, men, women, and children, seem to be in the streets with Union favors and flags; walking about uneasily, because their anxiety and nervous excitement will not permit them to stay at home. . . . Public meetings are held everywhere, in the small towns and villages as much as in the cities; considerable sums of money are voted to sustain the movement and take care of the families of those who are mustered into service. . . . Nobody holds back. Civil war is freely accepted everywhere; by some with alacrity, as the only means of settling a controversy based on long-cherished hatreds; by others as something sent as a judgment from Heaven, like a flood or an earthquake; by all as inevitable, by all as the least of the evils among which we are permitted to choose.

FROM

From Paul Burns's Letter to a Missouri Friend

JUNE 1861

Arrived in my old state of Tennessee and never saw the like. Men women & children are imbued with the spirit of war. There are over 80 thousand under arms in this state & men swair *[sic]* that they will not submit if it costs the last man in the state. I can hear the fife and drum from morning until night & see men in [uniform] all day & every railroad car that comes into town crowded with soldiers. . . . There are thousands of soldiers passing through this State every day from the South on their way to Virginia. . . .

Ann it makes my heart sick to think of the State of our once happy and yet beloved country for there is no history that tells of any country that was happier than ours—and now to see two brave and warlike armys armed with all the deadly instruments that art and wealth could procure marching over our once peaceful country and to think when they meet in the bloody battle fields what destruction and what misery they can produce.

Fort Sumter: The Opening Shots

Even after Lincoln took office in March 1861, there was still some hope that a compromise could be found to save the Union without bloodshed. Then a crisis developed over Fort Sumter, a federal fort located in the harbor of Charleston, South Carolina. Confederate leaders said that any attempt to reinforce the fort would be considered an act of war and Confederate cannons would blast the fort into surrender from the shore.

Lincoln insisted on the government's right to send food and supplies to the fort. When the Confederates were informed of this, they told the fort's commander, Major Robert Anderson, that he had until dawn on April 13, 1861, to surrender to Confederate forces. When Anderson refused, the Rebel cannons opened fire. The Civil War had begun.

The following selections include a report in an Ohio newspaper that presents the news as many Americans received it, and Captain Abner Doubleday's description of the shelling of the fort and the evacuation by the Union troops.

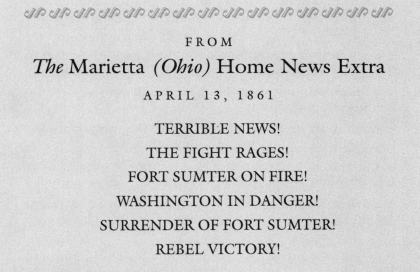

FROM

The Marietta *(Ohio)* Home News Extra

APRIL 13, 1861

TERRIBLE NEWS!

THE FIGHT RAGES!

FORT SUMTER ON FIRE!

WASHINGTON IN DANGER!

SURRENDER OF FORT SUMTER!

REBEL VICTORY!

The Fleet to Enter the Harbor

The opinion prevails that an attempt will be made before sunrise to run the eight . . . vessels of the fleet up to Fort Sumter to reenforce Major Anderson and also supply him with provisions.

The Battle Still Raging

The cannonading is going on fiercely from all points, from the vessels outside and all along the coast. It is reported that Fort Sumter is on fire.

Fort Sumter on Fire!

The roof of Fort Sumter is in a sheet of blaze. Major Anderson has ceased firing to extinguish it. Two of his magazines have exploded. The shells are flying over and around Fort Sumter in quick succession.

Rebels and Yankees

Confederate troops were nicknamed Rebels probably because the act of secession was officially called an act of rebellion. Northerners had long been known as Yankees, so that was a natural nickname for Union troops. The soldiers on each side were also referred to as "Johnny Reb" and "Billy Yank."

FROM

The Memoirs of Captain Abner Doubleday

APRIL 1861

As soon as the outline of our fort could be distinguished [at dawn on April 13, 1861], the enemy [opened fire]. . . . Almost immediately afterward a ball from Cummings Point lodged in the **magazine** wall and by the sound seemed to bury itself in the masonry about a foot from my head, in very unpleasant proximity to my right ear. . . .

By 11 A.M. the conflagration was terrible and disastrous. One fifth of the fort was on fire, and the wind drove the smoke in dense masses into the angle where we had all taken refuge. It seemed impossible to escape suffocation. Some lay down close to the ground with handkerchiefs over their mouths, and others posted themselves near the [openings], where the smoke was somewhat lessened by the draught of air. Every one suffered severely. . . . Had not a slight change of wind taken place, the result might have been fatal to most of us. . . .

[When further resistance was impossible, arrangements were made for Major Anderson to surrender Fort Sumter; he and his men were then allowed to march out of the fort and onto a Union supply ship sent to take them off.]

The next morning, Sunday, the 14th, we were up early, packing our baggage in readiness to go on the transport. The time having arrived, I made preparations, by order of Major Anderson, to fire a national salute to the flag. . . . The salute being over, the Confederate troops marched in to occupy the fort. . . .

Anderson directed me to form the men on the parade ground, assume command, and march them on board the transport. I told him I should prefer to leave the fort with the flag flying and the drums beating "Yankee Doodle," and

magazine: a storage area for gunpowder, ammunition, and explosives.

he authorized me to do so. As soon as our tattered flag came down and the silken banner made by the ladies of Charleston was run up, tremendous shouts of applause were heard from the vast multitude of spectators; and all the vessels and steamers, with one accord, made for the fort.

Abner Doubleday

Abner Doubleday served the Union cause well for the entire war and rose to the rank of major general. After the war, a legend grew that Doubleday had created the rules of baseball while living in Cooperstown, New York, before the war. There is little real proof of this, but the legend remained and was given official sanction by the Baseball Hall of Fame at Cooperstown.

The battered flag was preserved and restored to the ruins of the fort at the end of the war.

The interior of Fort Sumter, April 14, 1861, after the Union force under Major Robert Anderson had evacuated. The new Confederate flag already flies above the battered fort.

COURTESY NATIONAL ARCHIVES

*B*rother against Brother, Family against Family

Throughout America, thousands of families received the stunning news of the firing on Fort Sumter. Reactions ranged from shock and sadness to excitement. Many families discovered that they were far from united in their feelings about the war, and almost everyone had friends or relatives who were now enemies. The tragedy of these deep divisions is revealed in the next reading, as sixteen-year-old Theodore Upson, an Indiana farmboy, struggled to understand.

FROM
Theodore Upson's Recollections
1861

Father and I were husking out some corn. We could not finish before it wintered up. When William Cory came across the field (he had been down after the mail) he was excited and said, "Jonathan, the Rebs have fired upon and taken Fort Sumter." Father got white and couldn't say a word.

William said, "The President will soon fix them. He has called for 75,000 men and is going to blockade their ports, and just as soon as those fellows find out that the North means business, they will get down off their high horse."

Father said little. We did not finish the corn and drove to the barn. Father left me to unload and put out the team and went to the house. After I had finished I went in to dinner. Mother said, "What is the matter with father?" He had gone right upstairs. I told her what we had heard. She went to him. After a while they came down. Father looked ten years older. We sat down to the table. Grandma wanted to know what was the trouble. Father told her and she began to cry: "Oh, my poor children in the South! Now they will suffer! God knows how they will suffer! I knew it would come! Jonathan, I told you it would come!"

Family First

Robert E. Lee of Virginia was considered the country's best military leader and the Lincoln government offered him command of all Union armies. Lee reluctantly refused and chose to resign from the U.S. Army because Virginia had voted to secede and Lee's family and home were in Virginia. In a letter to Lincoln's secretary of war, Lee wrote, "I cannot raise my hand against my birthplace, my home, my children."

"They can come here and stay," said Father.

"No, they will not do that. There is their home. There they will stay. Oh, to think that I should have lived to see the day when Brother should rise against Brother."

She and Mother were crying and I lit out for the barn. I do hate to see women cry. . . .

We had another meeting at the schoolhouse last night; we are raising money to take care of the families of those who enlist. A good many gave money, others subscribed. . . . Mother had a letter from the Hales. Charlie and his father are in their army and Dayton wanted to go but was too young. I wonder if I were in our army and they should meet me would they shoot me. I suppose they would.

Deep Divisions

The clash of loyalties split families, communities, and states. The Union armies included men from every Southern state, and the Confederate forces included Northerners from throughout the Union. Several slave states remained in the Union—Missouri, Kentucky, Maryland, and Delaware—with the result that bitter fighting was needed to keep Missouri and Kentucky in the Union. In Maryland, mobs even attacked a Massachusetts regiment on its way to Washington. In addition, when Virginia voted to secede, six western counties broke away and applied for admission to the Union as the free state of West Virginia.

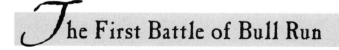

The First Battle of Bull Run

After Fort Sumter fell, neither government had any idea what to expect. Lincoln and his advisers decided that the quickest way to end the "insurrection" was to march south from Washington, D.C., and capture the new Confederate capital of Richmond, Virginia, only 110 miles away. "On to Richmond!" became the federal rallying cry. As raw recruits began the first drills at camps scattered around Washington, spirits were high. Bands played. Crowds gathered around the parade grounds. Then came the shock of battle.

By mid-July 1861, the federal army, called the Army of the Potomac, was on the move. Union general Irwin McDowell marched south toward Richmond, with 35,000 half-trained troops. The Confederate defenders under General P. G. T. Beauregard were waiting at a narrow stream called Bull Run, near the town of Manassas Junction, Virginia. As McDowell's troops struggled through the steamy July heat, crowds of spectators from Washington followed on the hills flanking the road. Many of the carriages carried elegant picnic lunches.

The fighting began before dawn on July 21, 1861, when McDowell ordered his forces to attack. For most of the day the inexperienced Yankee soldiers and officers fought well and, by mid-afternoon, seemed to have the battle won. A Confederate doctor, J. C. Nott, describes this part of the battle in the first selection following. Confederate reinforcements under General Joe Johnston began arriving by railroad from Winchester, Virginia, however, and as they rushed into the battle the Union troops

LIBRARY OF CONGRESS

Bull Run Creek, a Union cavalry patrol at one of the shallow crossings, several months after the July 1861 battle.

were forced to retreat. An overturned wagon blocking a bridge turned the retreat into panic, and the Union troops' disastrous flight from the battlefield is described in the second selection, by British journalist William Russell.

꠷ꠥ ꠷ꠥ ꠷ꠥ ꠷ꠥ ꠷ꠥ ꠷ꠥ ꠷ꠥ ꠷ꠥ ꠷ꠥ ꠷ꠥ ꠷ꠥ ꠷ꠥ ꠷ꠥ ꠷ꠥ

FROM
Dr. Nott's Letter to a Friend
JULY 23, 1861

When we arrived on the top of a hill, in an old field, we could get glimpses of the fight through the woods. The cannons were roaring and the musketry sounded like a large bundle of fire crackers, and the constant roaring of the big guns, the sharp sound of rifled cannons, **Minié rifles** and muskets, with the bursting of shells, made one feel that death was doing his work with fearful rapidity.

The [Union army] had concentrated all their forces on this one point while ours were scattered around a half-circle of ten miles, and the few regiments who received the first onset were most terribly cut up. It was far greater odds than human nature could stand, the regiments were torn to pieces, driven back, and so overwhelmed by numbers that I feared the day was lost. At this stage of the game the enemy was telegraphing to Washington that the battle had been won, and secession was about to be crushed. My heart failed me as I saw load after load of our poor wounded and dying soldiers brought and strewed on the ground, along the ravine where I was at work. . . .

At this juncture I saw [Johnston's] reinforcements pouring in with the rapidity and eagerness of a fox chase, and was satisfied that they would drive everything before them. No one can imagine such a grand, glorious picture as these patriots presented, rushing to the field through the masses of wounded bodies which strewed the roadside as they passed along.

"Like a Stone Wall!"

At the peak of the federal advances midway through the battle, the Confederate troops seemed ready to panic and run. At that moment, General Bernard Bee saw the brigade of General Thomas J. Jackson holding their position firmly at the crest of a hill. "Look!" General Bee shouted, "There is Jackson standing like a stone wall! Rally behind the Virginians!" The Rebels held and reversed the tide of the battle. From that moment on, Jackson was known as "Stonewall Jackson."

Minié rifle: a rifle that shot a special cone-shaped bullet with a hollow base. This minié (pronounced min-ee-aye) bullet expanded when fired to fit the grooves or rifles of a gun, which propelled the bullet with greater force and gave it more killing power.

Torpedoes

Another new device in naval warfare was the torpedo. Actually, Civil War torpedoes were what would be called mines today. These devices were filled with gunpowder, and small tubes projecting from the sides were filled with fulminate (a flame-producing substance) that touched off the gunpowder when struck. Some torpedoes were simply beer kegs filled with gunpowder.

FROM

The Account by William H. Russell

JULY 1861

[As the Union soldiers ran wildly in retreat, journalist Russell found himself swept along by the chaos.]

There was nothing left for it but to go with the current one could not stem. I turned round my horse. . . . I was unwillingly approaching Centerville in the midst of heat, dust, confusion, [pleas] inconceivable. . . . The ground over which I had passed going out was now covered with arms, clothing of all kinds, accouterments thrown off and left to be trampled under the hoofs of men and horses. The runaways ran alongside the waggons, striving to force themselves in among the occupants, who resisted tooth and nail. . . .

[Back in Washington] I saw a steady stream of men covered with mud, soaked through with rain, who were pouring irregularly, without any semblance of order, up Pennsylvania Avenue towards the Capitol. A dense stream of vapor rose from the multitude; but looking closely at the men, I perceived they belonged to different regiments, New Yorkers, Michiganders, Rhode Islanders, Massachusetters, Minnesotians, mingled pellmell together. . . .

The news seemed incredible. But there, before my eyes, were the jaded, dispirited, broken remnants of regiments passing onwards where and for what I know not, and it was evident enough that the mass of the grand army of the Potomac was placing that river between it and the enemy as rapidly as possible.

The Duel of the Ironclads

One of the most famous sea battles in history involved just two ships, and very strange-looking ships at that. Here is how it came about.

As soon as the war began, Lincoln ordered a naval blockade of the entire Confederate coastline. The goal was to prevent the South from shipping cotton to Europe to exchange for weapons and other supplies.

The South had no navy when the war began. They built a few ships as "blockade runners" and they bought a few warships in England that they used to attack Union supply ships. The greatest hope of the Confederates was in a large ship named the *Merrimac,* captured from the North. Southern engineers covered it with thick iron plates, creating a monstrous-looking vessel that awestruck Northerners called "The Thing." (The Confederates renamed it the *Virginia,* but most people then, and now, continued to call it the *Merrimac.*)

When the steam-powered ironclad lumbered into action on March 8, 1862, it looked to be unstoppable. In just four hours, the *Merrimac* easily defeated four Union ships, while enemy shells bounced off its six-inch-thick iron plates. Fear gripped Washington, D.C.

But the Union shipyards had also been working on an ironclad, a ship with a revolving gun turret designed by naval inventor John Ericsson. Observers said that Ericsson's *Monitor* looked like "a round cheese on a board." The day after the *Merrimac*'s victorious debut, the *Monitor* steamed into the waters of Chesapeake Bay. In the five-hour battle that followed neither ship could sink the other.

Although the battle was a draw, it ended the South's dream that the *Merrimac* would control Chesapeake Bay, enabling blockade runners to sail in or out of the bay without opposition.

Within a year, both of history's first ironclads were gone. Unable to get the *Merrimac* out to sea, the Rebels burned it, rather than let it fall into Union hands. The *Monitor* sank during a storm. Their one famous battle ushered in the age of steel-hulled warships.

In July 2002, salvage crews located the sunken *Monitor* and managed to raise the gun turret to the surface.

COURTESY NATIONAL ARCHIVES

The Monitor *after the battle with the* Merrimac. *The turret shows dents from sharp-nosed cannon shells.*

PART IV

STALEMATE EAST AND WEST

Bull Run sent a great shock wave through the North. People felt humiliated by the defeat, and they were stunned to discover that the Rebels were going to be a tough fighting force. At the same time, however, the battle made many Confederates dangerously overconfident.

Throughout late 1861 and all of 1862, Americans were repeatedly shocked into realizing that this war was not going to be short and that it was going to be far bloodier than anyone had dreamed possible. In fact, by late 1862, more soldiers had been killed than in all of America's previous wars combined, from the colonial period through the Mexican War (1846–1848).

During these months from Bull Run until 1862, the war settled into a tense stalemate—a period when neither side could gain a decisive advantage over the other. Both sides built up their military forces and began probing for weak spots in the enemy. The federal leadership developed a three-pronged attack to bring down the Rebel government. One part was the naval blockade, designed to choke off supplies from Europe. Second, the goal of the land war in the East was for the Army of the Potomac to move south through Virginia and capture Richmond. The third route of attack was in the West, where Union forces would attempt to gain control of the entire Mississippi River, cutting off the western states of the Confederacy from the states of the East.

The readings in part IV provide information about what the war was like during the long period of stalemate.

Experiencing War Firsthand

Between 1861 and 1865, roughly 3 million Americans experienced the Civil War firsthand. The two readings that follow offer reactions to two different aspects of war. In the first selection, a young man who survived four years of warfare describes his first experiences of military life. The second selection presents Abner Small's first encounter on the battlefield.

FROM

The Recollections of Warren Lee Goss

1890

Cold chills ran up and down my back as I got out of bed after a sleepless night, and shaved preparatory to other desperate deeds of valor. I was twenty years of age, and when anything unusual was to be done, like fighting or courting, I shaved.

With a nervous tremor convulsing my system, and my heart thumping like muffled drumbeats, and before turning the knob to enter, read and reread the advertisement for recruits. . . . The promised chances for "travel and promotion" seemed good, and I thought I might have made a mistake in considering war so serious after all. "Chances for travel!" I must confess now, after four years of soldiering, that the chances for travel were no myth; but "promotion" was a little uncertain and slow. . . .

My first uniform was a bad fit. My trousers were too long by three or four inches; the flannel shirt was coarse and unpleasant, too large at the neck and too short elsewhere. The forage cap was an ungainly bag with pasteboard top and leather visor; the blouse was the only part which seemed decent; while the overcoat made me feel like a little nubbin of corn in a large preponderance of husk. . . .

The first day I went out to drill, getting tired of doing the same things over and over, I said to the drill sergeant: "Let's stop this fooling and go over to the grocery." His only reply was addressed to a corporal: "Corporal, take this man out and drill him like hell"; and the corporal did! I found that suggestions were not so well appreciated in the army as in private life, and that no wisdom was equal to a drillmaster's.

Confederate troops attacking a Union position.

FROM

The Memoirs of Major Abner R. Small

1861

The next thing we knew, we were in the field on a hill and facing the enemy. I can only recall that we stood there and blazed away. There was a wild uproar of shouting and firing. The faces near me were inhuman. From somewhere across the field a **battery** pounded us; in the hot, still air the smoke of the cannon clung to the ground before it lifted; and through the smoke, straight ahead of us, flashed and crackled the Rebel musketry. We didn't see our foes; they were obscured in smoke and trees. We felt that our lines were needlessly exposed, and weak without cannon to return blow for blow. David Bates, one of my close companions, was smashed by a solid shot; and what reply could we make to that? We wavered and rallied, and fired blindly; and men fell writhing, and others melted from sight; and we saw the glitter of bayonets coming against our flank; and we hear the order to retire. It was the turn of the tide for this battle.

battery: a cannon.

The First Campaign for Richmond

After the Union disaster at Bull Run, President Lincoln replaced General McDowell as commander of the Army of the Potomac with General George McClellan. The president's orders were simple: train the soldiers so they would fight rather than run, then march on Richmond and capture it. Nearly ten months passed before McClellan felt ready to move on Richmond, the Confederate capital. Rather than march south, he had his army transported by ship to the Yorktown Peninsula, then moved north-west toward Richmond.

At the first Battle of Bull Run, in July 1861, each army had numbered about 30,000 men. In the summer of 1862, McClellan's well-drilled Army of the Potomac had 105,000 men. Opposing this huge army, the Confederates had about 85,000 men, commanded by General Robert E. Lee, who named his fighting force the Army of Northern Virginia. These two armies were destined to battle it out in the East until the end of the war in April 1865.

People throughout the country were amazed at the huge numbers now in uniform, and they were shocked by the enormous number of casualties during the first campaign for Richmond. In a series of battles known as the Seven Days, Lee's army sustained 20,000 casualties—killed, wounded, or missing. This meant that roughly 24 percent of the men who entered the battle became casualties. Union losses for this seven-day battle were slightly less—16,000 total casualties. Horrifying as these casualties were, Americans would soon be trying to adjust to far higher numbers.

In the selection that follows, Alexander Hunter describes the scene in Richmond, Virginia, while McClellan's Union forces hammered at the city's outskirts in the summer of 1862. Hunter was a private in a Virginia regiment.

FROM

The Recollections of Alexander Hunter

1862

In the city, busy, bustling and sad enough scenes were being enacted on every side. New regiments from the far South had just arrived and were marching through the streets, cheering and waving their hats as they passed; batteries of artillery were defiling along the thoroughfares, the drivers cracking their whips and urging their horses into a trot, all

Lee's Surprising Victory

Although the Union forces advanced within sight of Richmond, they could not break through the stubborn defenses of the Army of Northern Virginia. McClellan, convinced that his Army of the Potomac was outnumbered (it wasn't), ordered his men to retreat to the James River and they were ferried back to Washington, D.C. Southerners cheered the saving of Richmond and Lee became the South's great hero.

going toward the front. . . . Long lines of ambulances coming from the opposite way toiled slowly along, filled with the wounded from the battlefield, who were being carried to the various city hospitals—the long, torturing way marked by the trail of blood that oozed drop by drop from the human veins within, or else might be seen a wagonload of dead piled one upon another, their stiffened, rigid feet exposed to view, showing to the horrified spectator that for just so many the cares and sorrows of this life, its pain and misery, were passed forever.

. . . The more slightly wounded were made to walk, and long lines of them could be seen hobbling along the street, their wounds bound up in bloody rags. The citizens turned out in full force and did all in their power to alleviate this suffering; there was scarcely a house in Richmond wherein some wounded were not taken to be nursed with tenderest care; indeed, in some instances parlors and passages as well as chambers were converted into temporary hospitals, and everything done that unwearied nursing and gentlest attention could devise, and that for the roughest soldiers in the ranks as readily as for the highest general who wore his stars. Ladies stood in front of their homes with **waiters** of food and drink, luxuries and wine, which they dealt out unsparingly to the wounded soldiers that passed them.

The people realized with a sudden shock the actualities of a [civil war] and it was brought to their very doors. Before, they had seen only its pride and pomp, and a martial showing; they had only heard the rattling of artillery over the stony streets, and the tread of passing columns; but all at once, with the sound of hostile guns, gaunt, grim-visaged war touched their hearts, and sickened their souls with horror. . . . In one day Richmond was changed from a mirth-loving, pleasure-seeking city into a city resolute and nerved to make any sacrifice for the cause she loved.

waiters: serving trays.

The Development of Modern Weapons

Improvements in weapons contributed to the alarmingly high casualty figures. Rifles and cannons became much more effective killing machines, for example. Both were now equipped with rifled, or grooved, barrels. The grooves gave the bullet or ball a spin that sent it out the barrel in a straighter, more accurate line. Another change was the perfection of repeating rifles. The Union had these first, allowing the federal soldier to fire five or six shots, while his enemy could shoot only once, then had to reload.

A Union mortar battery. These squat-looking guns were called Napoleons, and artillery officers praised their effectiveness. The mortar was designed to shoot in a high arc, then explode above enemy lines, raining fragments over a wide area.

The Military Leaders

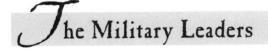

Battlefield leadership was of critical importance in the Civil War. Generals were now in command of armies numbering more than 100,000 men. On the march, with their artillery and supply wagons, an army could stretch out for twenty miles or more. In addition to working out battle strategies, the generals and their staffs had to know where each unit of their army was and how to move it to where it was needed when it was needed. The first battle at Bull Run had been fought in mass confusion and the commanders on both sides had made tragic blunders. The leaders who replaced them were determined to learn from these mistakes.

During the eighteen months following Bull Run, several brilliant Confederate leaders emerged, including Generals Robert E. Lee, Thomas

"Stonewall" Jackson, and J. E. B. Stuart, the cavalry genius. The Union was not as fortunate. Lincoln had to rely on General George B. McClellan and others until General Ulysses S. Grant began to take charge in the West in 1862.

The following selections offer eyewitness assessments of each of these men. They became larger-than-life figures who added to the colorful drama of the war.

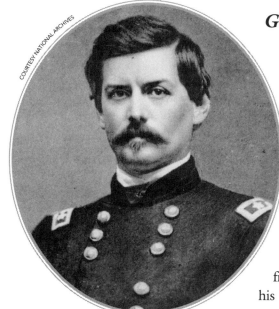

COURTESY NATIONAL ARCHIVES

*Union general
George B. McClellan.*

General George B. McClellan

General McClellan was a handsome, dashing soldier, immensely popular with his men. He spent months drilling his troops and transformed the Army of the Potomac into a disciplined, efficient army. But then he became reluctant to commit his army in battle, stalling often, and asking for more men and equipment. Finally, in the summer of 1862, he had the army moved by sea to the Yorktown Peninsula and marched north toward Richmond. In a series of bloody battles, the federals reached the outskirts of Richmond, but then McClellan withdrew to the James River. In the following fragments from this time, he reveals his habit of blaming others for his own failings.

McClellan's Popularity

General McClellan remained popular with the soldiers, even after he was removed from command. One Union soldier wrote in a letter home, "No general could ask for greater love and more unbounded confidence than he receives from his men. . . . He is everywhere among 'his boys,' as he calls them, and everywhere he is received with the most unbounded enthusiasm."

In 1864, McClellan ran for the presidency against Lincoln and, for a time, it seemed he might win. But a series of Union victories persuaded voters to stay with Lincoln.

FROM

General McClellan's Dispatches to Washington, D.C.

1862

The Rebel force is stated to be 200,000, including Jackson [it was actually less than half that number]. . . . I shall have to continue against vastly superior odds. . . . If this Army is destroyed by overwhelming numbers . . . the responsibility cannot be thrown on my shoulders; it must rest where it belongs.

[After a defeat at Gaines' Mill, Virginia, June 27, 1862] I have lost this battle because my force was too small. . . . The Government has not sustained this army. . . . If I save this army now, I tell you plainly that I owe no thanks to you or to any other persons in Washington.

Confederate general Robert E. Lee.

General Robert E. Lee

While the war produced many great figures, North and South, General Robert E. Lee stood head and shoulders above the other soldiers. He took command of the Confederate army defending Richmond in June 1862, when the army's commander, General Joseph Johnston, was wounded. A South Carolina officer, General Evander M. Law, describes his first glimpse of Lee the day he took command.

COURTESY NATIONAL ARCHIVES

FROM

General Law's Account of Robert E. Lee

1862

General Lee had up to this time accomplished nothing to warrant the belief in his future greatness as a commander. . . . There was naturally a good deal of speculation among the soldiers as to how he would "pan out." The general tone, however, was one of confidence invariably strengthened by a sight of the man himself. Calm, dignified, and commanding in his bearing, a countenance strikingly benevolent and self-possessed, a clear, honest eye that could look a friend or enemy in the face . . . simply and neatly dressed in the uniform of his rank, felt hat, and top boots reaching to the knee; sitting his horse as if his home was in the saddle; such was Robert E. Lee . . . when he assumed command . . . in June 1862, never to relinquish it for a day, until its colors were furled for ever at Appomattox.

Confederate general J. E. B. (Jeb) Stuart.

COURTESY NATIONAL ARCHIVES

General J. E. B. (Jeb) Stuart

Cavalry units were rarely used for direct charges in a battle. Instead, their main roles were to scout the enemy's strength and position, to form a screen to protect a flank, or side, of the army, and to conduct raids behind enemy lines. Jeb Stuart was a master of all these tasks and, for the first two years of the war, he constantly kept the Union armies off balance. Lee loved him like a son and used him wisely for swift, hammerlike blows.

Stuart was called "Beauty" because of the handsome, dashing figure he cut. He wore knee-high cavalry boots, elbow-length gloves, a red-lined cape with a yellow sash, and a felt hat with the brim turned up to hold an ostrich-feather plume. This heroic image, however, was tarnished in 1863 when he failed Lee on the eve of the Battle of Gettysburg, and that failure may have cost the Confederates any chance of winning that crucial conflict.

In the following reading, young Sallie Putnam describes watching him lead the troopers through Richmond in June 1862.

FROM

The Observations of Sallie Putnam

JUNE 1862

Through our streets poured our cavalry, under their gallant chieftain, the pink of Southern Chivalry—the gay, rollicking, yet bold, daring and venturous "Jeb" Stuart. As we saw him then, sitting easily on his saddle, as though he was born to it, he seemed every inch the cavalier. His stout yet lithe figure, his graceful bearing . . . his bright, beaming countenance . . . his dark red hair and flowing beard, with his lower limbs encased in cavalry boots, made up the *tout ensemble* of this brave son of Maryland. His genial temperament made him the idol and companion of the most humble of his men, and his deeds of daring made him respected as their leader.

With 1,200 troopers in his cavalry division, Stuart made a complete circle around McClellan's army of 100,000 during the first campaign for Richmond, in 1862. McClellan, desperate to locate the elusive Stuart, sent a Union cavalry regiment to find him. The Union force, which happened to be commanded by Stuart's father-in-law, General Philip St. George, never did find the 1,200-man regiment.

COURTESY NATIONAL ARCHIVES

Confederate general Thomas "Stonewall" Jackson.

General Thomas "Stonewall" Jackson

By late summer 1862, Lee's Army of Northern Virginia had stopped McClellan's drive on Richmond, and Lee felt ready to go on the offensive. To accomplish this, he used the daring strategy of dividing his army, sending Stonewall Jackson's corps on a wide flanking motion to get to the rear of the enemy. Few commanders would dare such a maneuver—if the federal forces spotted the move, they could attack Lee's weakened army first, then go after Jackson. But Lee counted on McClellan's cautious nature and he had great confidence in Jackson. In the following selection, Confederate Major Robert Dabney describes the first part of Jackson's race around the Union army.

FROM

Robert L. Dabney's The Life and Campaigns of Lt. General Thomas J. Jackson

1866

His troops had been constantly marching and fighting for five days; many of them had no rations, and subsisted on the green corn gathered along the route; yet their indomitable enthusiasm and devotion knew no flagging. As the weary column approached the end of the day's march, they found Jackson, who had ridden forward, dismounted, and was standing upon a great stone by the road-side. . . .

His men burst forth into the accustomed cheers, forgetting all their fatigue at his inspiring presence; but . . . he sent an officer to request that there should be no cheering inasmuch it might betray their presence to the enemy. They at once repressed their applause. . . . But as they passed him, their eyes and gestures, eloquent with suppressed affection, silently declared what their lips were forbidden to utter. Jackson turned to his Staff, his face beaming with delight, and said: "Who could not conquer with such troops as these?"

General Ulysses S. Grant

Ulysses S. Grant was the only general on either side who came at all close to Lee's reputation. When the war began, however, Grant had not even been in the army. Like many of the generals, both Union and Confederate, Grant had graduated from West Point and he had served well in the war with Mexico, but his career stagnated after that war, and rumors of his heavy drinking made it difficult for him to earn a promotion. Grant resigned from the army, then struggled to find a career in civilian life. When the Civil War began, he was given a chance to command a small force in the West. Early in 1862, he gave the Union its first two victories. First, in a combined operation with navy gunboats, he forced the surrender of Fort Henry on the Tennessee River, then he attacked Fort Donelson on the Cumberland with the same result.

The following selection is from a newspaper article written after the war, which tells how Grant knew it was time to attack Fort Donelson.

Union general Ulysses S. Grant.

ℐℐ ℐℐ ℐℐ ℐℐ ℐℐ ℐℐ ℐℐ ℐℐ ℐℐ ℐℐ ℐℐ ℐℐ ℐℐ ℐℐ ℐℐ

FROM

The New York Daily Tribune

1885

The attack on Fort Donelson, which established Grant's fame, is said to have been decided upon by a simple circumstance. The day before the attack [on February 15, 1862], most of the troops had marched a long distance, part of it in a bitter cold night. A council of war was called to determine whether an immediate attack should be made, or whether the troops should have a day of rest. The officers were in favor of rest. Grant said nothing, but appeared absorbed in thought. Presently, when everyone had expressed an opinion, he said: "There was a deserter came in this morning. Let us see him and hear what he has to say." The man was sent for and came in. Grant looked in his **haversack** and then asked: "Where are you from?"

"Fort Donelson."

"Got six days' rations in your haversack, have you not?"

"Yes, sir."

"When were they served out?"

"Yesterday morning."

"The same to all the troops?"

"Yes, sir."

The soldier was sent out and Grant said: "Gentlemen, troops do not have six days' rations served out to them if they mean to stay there. These men mean to retreat—not to fight. We will attack at once."

haversack: knapsack.

Grant and Lincoln

Only a year after Grant's success against Forts Henry and Donelson, he came under heavy criticism for his high casualty numbers and rumors of his binge drinking. Grant may have suffered from alcoholism but that has never been firmly established. Even when his reputation was lowest, President Lincoln stood by him. Early in 1863, Lincoln said, "I think Grant has hardly a friend left, except myself. . . . What I want is generals who will fight battles and win victories. Grant has done this and I propose to stand by him."

Camp Life

The actual fighting of battles and moving to new locations usually occupied little of a soldier's time. Most of his time was spent in camp, where life could be extremely boring. Drills kept the men sharp and disciplined, but the daily routine was tedious. The following reading is a young New Yorker's account of camp life.

FROM

Lawrence Van Alstyne's Diary

SEPTEMBER 1862

September 17, 1862. Maybe I have described our life here before, but as no one description can do it justice I am going to try again. We are in a field of 100 acres, as near as I can judge, on the side of a hill, near the top. . . . We sleep in pairs, and a blanket spread on the ground is our bed while another spread over us is our covering. A narrow strip of muslin, drawn over a pole about three feet from the ground, open at both ends, the wind and rain, if it does rain, beating in upon us, and water running under and about us; this, with all manner of bugs and creeping things crawling over us, and all the while great hungry mosquitoes biting every uncovered inch of us, is not an overdrawn picture of that part of a soldier's life, set apart for the rest and repose necessary to enable him to endure several hours of . . . hard work at drill, in a hot sun with heavy woolen clothes on, every button of which must be tight-buttoned, and by the time the officers are tired of watching us, we come back to camp wet through with perspiration and too tired to make another move. . . .

The [kitchen] is simply a portion of the field we are in. . . . The camp kettles are large sheet-iron pails, one larger

Camp Stores

Supply outfits, called *sutlers*, set up tents on the edge of army camps. They sold food and tobacco at outrageous prices, but soldiers who had a little money welcomed the chance to buy some fruit, milk, old newspapers, or other luxuries. Since most of the fighting took place in the South, the Confederates had easier access to supplies, at least early in the war. And, in the early months, some Southern gentlemen arrived in camp with their own cooks and servants.

than the other so one can be put inside the other when moving. If we have meat and potatoes, meat is put in one and potatoes in the other. The one that gets cooked first is emptied into mess pans, which are large sheet-iron pans with flaring sides, so one can be packed in another. Then the coffee is put in the empty kettle and boiled. The bread is cut into thick slices, and the breakfast call sounds. We grab our plates and cups, and wait for no second invitation. We each get a piece of meat and a potato, a chunk of bread and a cup of coffee with a spoonful of brown sugar in it. Milk and butter we buy, or go without. We settle down, usually in groups, and the meal is soon over. Then we wash our dishes, and put them back in our haversacks. We make quick work of washing dishes. We save a piece of bread for the last, with which we wipe up everything, and then eat the dish rag. Dinner and breakfast are alike, only sometimes the meat and potatoes are cut up and cooked together, which makes a really delicious stew. Supper is the same, minus the meat and minus the potatoes.

Life in camp.

The Image of the Enemy

One of the most difficult aspects of the Civil War for modern readers to grasp is that the men who fought these incredibly violent battles did not hate their enemy. They fought with tremendous ferocity but without bitterness. Soldiers on both sides often demonstrated the greatest respect for each other.

A Civil War Song

Civil War troops sang when they marched, usually stirring, patriotic songs. One of the most famous is included here. "The Battle Hymn of the Republic" was written by a young wife and mother, Julia Ward Howe. Knowing her talent as a poet, some soldiers had asked her to write words to the popular tune called "John Brown's Body." By the next morning she had written the words for one of the most famous songs in America's history.

"The Battle Hymn of the Republic"

FEBRUARY 1862

Mine eyes have seen the glory of the coming of the Lord:
He is trampling out the vintage where the grapes of wrath
  are stored;
He hath loosed the fateful lightning of his terrible swift
  sword:
   His truth is marching on.

[Refrain:]
  Glory, glory Hallelujah,
  Glory, glory Hallelujah,

> Glory, glory Hallelujah,
>   His truth is marching on.
>
> I have seen Him in the watch fires of a hundred circling
>   camps;
> They have builded him an altar in the evening dews and
>   damps;
> I can read his righteous sentence by the dim and flaring
>   lamps.
>   His day is marching on.
>
> [Refrain]
>
> He has sounded forth the trumpet that shall never call
>   retreat;
> He is sifting out the hearts of men before his judgment
>   seat:
> Oh! be swift, my soul, to answer Him! be jubilant, my
>   feet!
>   Our God is marching on.
>
> [Refrain]
>
> In the beauty of the lilies Christ was born across the sea,
> With a glory in His bosom that transfigures you and me:
> As He died to make men holy, let us die to make men free,
>   While God is marching on.
>
> [Refrain]

Two Women Spies

Rose O'Neal Greenhow was considered the master Confederate spy. Attractive and intelligent, she was known as "the most persuasive woman in Washington," and managed to send vital information to Rebel leaders even when she was in jail. At the first Battle of Bull Run, the Confederate commander knew exactly when and where the Yankees would attack, thanks to her last-minute message. In the following selection, Greenhow describes the Union authorities' efforts to try her for treason. The second reading is a newspaper account of Belle Boyd, another great Rebel agent. She was jailed twice, then banished to England; on the ocean crossing, she fell in love with one of her guards and they were married.

FROM
Rose O'Neal Greenhow's Diary
MARCH 1862

General Dix turned over and over again the papers before him, which were my letters seized by the detective police, and which, though relevant to the subject matter, had no legal importance or bearing at this time. He selected one, laying his hand upon it, but still hesitated. I watched him keenly.

At last he said, "You are charged with treason."

"I deny it, sir. During the eight months of my imprisonment I have had ample time to study the Constitution of the United States, and there is no act or provision in it which will justify a charge of that nature against me."

"And so you deny the charge of treason?"

"I do, sir, most emphatically; and, moreover, report the charge against yourself as being the minister of a President who has violated the Constitution, destroyed the personal rights of the citizen, and inaugurated revolution. At this moment, sir, you are presiding at, and conducting a trial unlawful in every sense, and without even a pretence of the legal form prescribed; for the Constitution of the United States is very precise and specific as to the mode in which a trial for treason shall be conducted. It requires that the charge of treason shall be sustained by two respectable witnesses, which you could not find in all Yankeedom."

"You are charged, madam, with holding communication with the enemy in the South."

Rose O'Neal Greenhow with her daughter at Old Capital Prison in Washington.

"If this were an established fact, you could not be suprised at it. I am a Southern woman, and I thank God that no drop of Yankee blood ever polluted my veins; and as all that I have ever honored or respected have been driven by ruthless despotism to seek shelter there, it would seem the most natural thing in life that I should have done so."

"How is it, madam, that you have managed to communicate, in spite of the vigilance exercised over you?"

"That is my secret, sir; and, if it be any satisfaction to you to know it, I shall, in the next forty-eight hours, make a report to my Government at Richmond of this rather farcical trial of treason."

"General M'Clellan, madam, charges you with having obtained a thorough knowledge of his plans, and of forcing him consequently four times to change them."

At this I smilingly shrugged my shoulders, without replying, saying, "Well, what else?"

After a few moments General Dix said, "Governor, I think we have nothing else to say to Mrs. Greenhow?" To which Governor Fairfield replied, "No, sir, I think not."

The Loss of the "Lady Spy of Washington"

In 1864 Rose Greenhow went to England to raise money for the Confederate cause. She returned loaded with gold to aid the South. Some of the gold coins were sewn into her clothing, and that effort at secrecy cost her her life. When the ship tried to run the Yankee blockade it was sunk and came to rest on a sandbar. Mrs. Greenhow insisted on being rowed ashore, but the small boat capsized and she was drowned. The next morning, hundreds of glistening coins were washed ashore on the tide.

The New York Herald

AUGUST 1862

The notorious female spy, Belle Boyd, familiarly known as the betrayer of our forces at Front Royal . . . was arrested at Winchester on Wednesday last, and is now confined in the Old Capitol prison. Romancers have given this female undue repute by describing her as beautiful and educated. She is merely a brusque, talkative woman, perhaps twenty-five years of age, red-haired, with keen, courageous gray eyes. . . . Our young officers, dazzled, perhaps, took her out riding often, and she was frequently a [visitor] to our camps in the Shenandoah. From facts gleaned in this way of our movements and projects, she kept up a pretty regular budget of intelligence, and the enemy was advised of our favorite designs. She admitted in prison today that she had informed Jackson of our situation at Front Royal; but this, she said, was done to prevent the effusion of blood. . . . A leading secessionist of Washington visited her in jail today, where her quarters are comfortable, and gave her luxuries. Some gentlemen likewise waited upon her. She talked with them at random, and with much abandon, and said that she intended to be paroled. A soldier guards her room, and paces up and down continually before the door.

Her own admissions will convict her of being a spy. She was dressed today in a plain frock, low in the neck, and her arms were bare. . . . She takes her arrest as a matter of course, and is smart, plucky, and as absurd as ever. A lunatic asylum might be recommended for her.

LIBRARY OF CONGRESS

Allan Pinkerton, head of the famous Pinkerton Detective Agency, thwarted a plot to assassinate President Lincoln on his way to Washington in 1861. Then, disguised as Major E. J. Allen, he formed a department of counter-espionage attached to the Army of the Potomac.

Horace Greeley versus President Lincoln

From the start of the war, the North's most ardent abolitionists insisted that the president should immediately issue an Emancipation Proclamation declaring all slaves free. Lincoln hesitated for several reasons. First, many Northerners were willing to fight to put down a rebellion that threatened the Union, but not to free the slaves. Second, several slave states had remained in the Union—Maryland, Delaware, Kentucky, and Missouri. And third, there was no way to enforce emancipation in the states of the Confederacy; in fact, until Grant's triumphs over Forts Henry and Donelson, the Union had not won a battlefield victory.

A well-known newspaper editor, Horace Greeley, was outspoken in demanding that Lincoln act. The following selection is from Lincoln's famous reply.

FROM

Lincoln's Reply to Greeley

AUGUST 1862

If there be those who would not save the Union unless they could at the same time save slavery, I do not agree with them. If there be those who would not save the Union unless they could at the same time destroy slavery I do not agree with them. My paramount object in this struggle is to save the Union, and is not either to save or destroy slavery. If I could save the Union without freeing any slave, I would do it; if I could do it by freeing all the slaves, I would do it; and if I could do it by freeing some and leaving others alone, I would also do that. . . . I have here stated my purpose according to my view of official duty, and I intend no modification of my oft-expressed personal wish that all men, everywhere, could be free.

Antietam: The Bloodiest Day

Even before his exchange with Greeley, Lincoln had decided to issue an Emancipation Proclamation, which would free the slaves, but he accepted the advice of Secretary of State William Seward to wait until the Union had a battlefield victory. In September 1862, Lee's Army of Northern Virginia invaded the North by crossing the Potomac River into Maryland. The result was the Battle of Antietam, which turned out to be the bloodiest single day of fighting in the entire war. General McClellan's Army of the Potomac outnumbered the Rebels almost two to one, but the battle ended in what was essentially a draw. The Union, however, had forced Lee to give up his invasion and retreat into Virginia; Lincoln decided that was enough of a federal victory to justify issuing the Emancipation Proclamation.

The following two readings offer glimpses of the battle from a Union major's memoirs and from the account of Confederate general John B. Gordon, who survived to become a senator from Georgia.

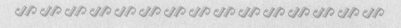

FROM

Union Major Rufus Dawes's Memoirs

1862

As we approached the edge of [a cornfield], a long line of men in butternut and gray rose up from the ground. Simultaneously, the hostile battle lines opened a tremendous fire upon each other. Men, I cannot say fell; they were knocked out of the ranks by dozens. But we jumped over the fence, and pushed on, loading, firing, and shouting as we advanced. There was, on the part of the men, great hysterical excitement, eagerness to go forward, and a reckless disregard of life, of everything but victory. . . .

Another line of our men came up through the corn. We

all joined together, jumped over the fence, and again pushed on into the open field. There is a rattling fusilade and loud cheers. "Forward!" is the word. The men are loading and firing with demoniacal fury and shouting and laughing hysterically, and the whole field before us is covered with Rebels fleeing for life into the woods.

FROM

General John B. Gordon's Reminiscences

1862

My extraordinary escapes from wounds in all the previous battles made a deep impression on my comrades as well as upon my own mind. So many had fallen at my side, so often had balls and shells pierced and torn my clothing, grazing my body without drawing a drop of blood, that a sort of blind faith possessed my men that I was not to be killed in battle. . . .

Then, at Sharpsburg [Antietam] the storm came and the whizzing Miniés began to pierce my body. The first volley from the Union lines in my front sent a ball through the brain of the chivalric Colonel Tew, of North Carolina, to whom I was talking, and another ball through the calf of my right leg. On the right and the left my men were falling under the death-dealing crossfire like trees in a hurricane. . . . Higher up on the same leg I was again shot, but still no bone was broken. I was able to walk along the line and give encouragement to my resolute riflemen, who were firing with the steadiness and coolness of soldiers in target practice. When later in the day the third ball pierced my left arm, tearing asunder the tendons and mangling the flesh, they caught sight of the blood running down my fingers, and these devoted and big-hearted men, while still loading their guns, pleaded with me to leave them and go to the rear [but] I could not consent to leave them in such a crisis. . . .

A fourth ball ripped through my shoulder, leaving its base and a wad of clothing in its track. I could still stand and walk, although the shocks and loss of blood left but little of my normal strength. I remembered the pledge to the commander [Lee] that we would stay there till the battle ended or night came. I looked at the sun. It moved very slowly; in fact it seemed to stand still. . . .

I had gone but a short distance when I was shot down by a fifth ball, which struck me squarely in the face, and passed out, barely missing the jugular vein. I fell forward and lay unconscious with my face in my cap; and it would seem that I might have been smothered by the blood running into my cap from this last wound but for the act of some Yankee who, as if to save my life, had at a previous hour during the battle, shot a hole through the cap, which let the blood out. I was borne on a litter to the rear, and recall nothing more till revived by stimulants at a late hour of the night.

The Casualties at Antietam

The Battle of Antietam—known as the Battle of Sharpsburg in the Confederate records—saw some of the most desperate fighting of the entire war. By late in the day, the grays were in retreat and the Union blues seemed about to break through to a victory that would virtually destroy Lee's army. But at the last moment, 2,500 Rebels, who had been at Harpers Ferry, suddenly appeared at the crest of a hill and charged into the Union line with the blood-curdling "Rebel yell." Lee's troops stiffened and held. The attack, and the battle, were over.

The battle casualties were the worst for any single day of the war. The North suffered 2,108 killed, 9,549 wounded, and 753 missing—a total of 12,410. The South's estimated loses were 2,700 killed, 9,024 wounded, and 2,000 missing, for a total of 13,724.

The Emancipation Proclamation

After Antietam, President Lincoln was bitterly disappointed that McClellan did not press his advantage and force Lee to surrender. But he still regarded the battle as enough of a victory to issue the Emancipation Proclamation. As of January 1, 1863, the document stated, all slaves in states still in rebellion would be declared "forever free." No slaves were actually set free by the statement because the eleven Confederate states were still "in rebellion." Since the border states that remained loyal to the Union were not mentioned in the document, slavery continued in those states. The actual freeing of slaves in the Confederate states would depend on the Union armies, which could free slaves as they moved into the South.

Many people thought the proclamation would have little impact, or might even upset Northerners who were not interested in the fate of African Americans. It soon became clear, however, that the proclamation actually gave the North a noble new purpose—freedom for the 4 million people who had been enslaved for so long. In addition, the announcement damaged the South's hope that England, eager for the South's cotton, would officially recognize the Confederacy as an independent nation and provide aid. Now that the Union troops were fighting for freedom, the English government was not likely to oppose that cause.

The following selection is from the proclamation.

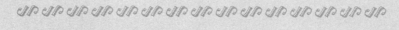

FROM

Lincoln's Emancipation Proclamation

SEPTEMBER 22, 1862

Whereas on the 22nd day of September, A.D. 1862, a proclamation was issued by the President of the United States, containing, among other things, the following, to wit:

"That on the 1st day of January, A.D. 1863, all persons held as slaves within any State or designated part of a State the people whereof shall then be in rebellion against the United States shall be then, thenceforward, and forever free; and the executive government of the United States, including the military and naval authority thereof, will recognize and maintain the freedom of such persons and will do no act or acts to repress such persons, or any of them, in any efforts they may make for their actual freedom. . . .

And I hereby enjoin upon the people so declared to be free to abstain from all violence, unless in necessary self-defence; and I recommend to them that, in all cases when allowed, they labor faithfully for reasonable wages.

And I further declare and make known that such persons of suitable condition will be received into the armed service of the United States to garrison forts, positions, stations, and other places, and to man vessels of all sorts in said service.

And upon this act, sincerely believed to be an act of justice, warranted by the Constitution upon military necessity, I invoke the considerate judgment of mankind and the gracious favor of Almighty God.

The first page of the Emancipation Proclamation.

African Americans in the War

Early in the war, Union forces captured the "Sea Islands" (including Hilton Head) off the coast of South Carolina. The islands gave them a base for controlling the port of Charleston and preventing Rebel blockade runners from reaching the open sea. Hundreds of slaves lived on the islands, or escaped to them, and many joined the first African American regiment being trained there. The regiment—the 54th Massachusetts—included free blacks from the North; the officers were white volunteers, including Robert Gould Shaw, the handsome son of a leading Boston family. A second regiment, the First South Carolina Volunteers, also trained on the islands and took part in the first battlefield action by black troops.

Another Northerner, Charlotte Forten, came to the islands to help educate the former slaves. Forten was a free African American, raised by a wealthy family and well educated. Her diary is one of the best accounts of the life of freed slaves during the war. The following readings present Forten's description of the celebration of the Emancipation Proclamation, and a letter by Lewis Douglass, one of the men in the 54th Massachusetts and the son of famous abolitionist Frederick Douglass.

FROM

Charlotte Forten's Diary

JANUARY 1863

New Year's Day, Emancipation Day, was a glorious one to us. General Saxton and Colonel Higginson had invited us to visit the camp of the First Regiment of South Carolina Volunteers on that day, "the greatest day in the nation's history." We enjoyed perfectly the exciting scene on board the steamboat *Flora*. There was an eager, wondering crowd of the freed people, in their holiday attire, with the gayest of headkerchiefs, the whitest of aprons and the happiest of faces. The band was playing, the flags were streaming, and everybody was talking merrily and feeling happy. . . .

The ceremony in honor of Emancipation took place in a beautiful grove of live-oaks adjoining the camp. . . . There were the black soldiers in their blue coats and scarlet pantaloons; the officers of the First Regiment, and of other regiments, in their handsome uniforms; and there were crowds of lookers-on, men, women, and children, of every complexion . . . under the moss-hung trees. The faces all wore a happy interested look.

The exercises began with a prayer by the chaplain of the regiment. An ode, written for the occasion, was then read and sung. President Lincoln's Proclamation of Emancipation was then read, and enthusiastically cheered. . . . After the meeting was over, we saw the dress-parade, which was a brilliant and beautiful sight. An officer told us that the men went through the drill remarkably well. . . . To us it seemed a strange miracle to see this regiment of blacks, the first mustered into the service of the United States, thus doing their honor in the sight of officers of other regiments, many of whom doubtless came to scoff. The men afterward had a great feast, ten oxen having been roasted whole.

"Forever free! forever free!"—those magical words from the President's Proclamation were constantly singing themselves in my soul.

The Attack on Fort Wagner

In July 1863, the 54th Massachusetts led an attack on Fort Wagner, one of several forts guarding Charleston. Although the attack failed, and roughly 40 percent of the six hundred men were casualties, the bravery they displayed lifted spirits throughout the North. Black soldiers had proved themselves when many had doubted they could stand up to battle. Colonel Shaw, their white officer, also set an example by leading the men over the wall into the fort, where he was quickly killed by a dozen wounds. He could have easily avoided serving with a black regiment.

The casualty list for the 54th Massachusetts Regiment after the assault on Fort Wagner, July 1863.

FROM

Lewis Douglass's Letter to His Fiancée

JULY 1863

My Dear Amelia:

I have been in two fights and am unhurt. I am about to go in another, I believe, tonight. Our men fought well on both occasions. The last was desperate—we charged that terrible battery on Morris Island known as Fort Wagner and were repulsed with a loss of [many] killed and wounded. I escaped unhurt from amidst that perfect hail of shot and shell. It was terrible. . . . Should I fall in the next fight killed or wounded, I hope to fall with my face to the foe. . . .

My regiment has established its reputation as a fighting regiment—not a man flinched, though it was a trying time. Men fell all around me. A shell would explode and clear a space of twenty feet. Our men would close up again, but it was no use; we had to retreat, which was a very hazardous undertaking. How I got out of that fight alive I cannot tell, but I am here. My dear girl, I hope again to see you. I must bid you farewell should I be killed. Remember, if I die, I die in a good cause. I wish we had a hundred thousand colored troops—we would put an end to this war.

PART V

*T*HE TURNING OF THE TIDE

The year 1863 witnessed the Civil War's great turning point. In the early months of the year, prospects for the Confederacy had never looked better. Lee's Army of Northern Virginia had recovered quickly from the damage of Antietam. Lee then led them to a stirring victory at the Battle of Fredericksburg, Virginia (December 1862) and another at Chancellorsville, Virginia (May 1863). At the same time, the Union forces in the West, now led by General Grant, had failed to capture Vicksburg, Mississippi, the South's last major stronghold on the Mississippi River.

The mood in the North was as gloomy as the South was buoyant. Demands for a truce to end the war grew louder every day. As the *Chicago Tribune* concluded, "An armistice is bound to come during the year '63. The Rebels can't be conquered by the present machinery."

The prospects for the South were so bright that Lee was permitted to launch a new invasion of the North, this time into Pennsylvania. Confederate

85

leaders were confident that this would strengthen the Northern demands for peace and might persuade England to recognize the independence of the Confederacy.

The picture changed with dramatic suddenness. By July 4, Lee's bold invasion was turned back at Gettysburg and Grant forced Vicksburg to surrender. Their hopes shattered, the Rebel troops staggered back to Virginia and searched for the spirit to carry on.

The readings in this part describe the dramatic events of 1863.

The Battle of Fredericksburg

After Antietam, in September 1862, President Lincoln became increasingly frustrated with McClellan's failure to follow through and drive for Richmond while the enemy was disorganized. Finally he removed McClellan and replaced him with General Ambrose Burnside. At the Battle of Fredericksburg in December 1862, however, Burnside made one of the great blunders of the war. He ordered his troops to attack up a slope called Marye's Heights directly into the Confederates' protected artillery and infantry. The Union army suffered a demoralizing defeat and Burnside was soon replaced by General "Fighting Joe" Hooker.

The two selections following present a Confederate soldier's account of the attack on Marye's Heights and a Union officer's recollection of the same scene.

FROM

Confederate William Owens's Account

DECEMBER 1862

At dawn . . . I stepped upon the [porch of a house some officers were using] overlooking the heights back of the little old-fashioned town of Fredericksburg. Heavy fog and mist hid the whole plain between the heights and the Rappahannock [River], but under cover of that fog and within easy cannon-shot lay Burnside's army. Along the heights, to the right and left of where I was standing, extending a length of nearly five miles, lay Lee's army. . . .

As the fog cleared around 12 o'clock . . . the enemy . . . showed himself above the crest of the ridge and advanced in columns, and at once our guns began their deadly work with shell and solid shot. How beautifully they came on! Their bright bayonets glistening in the sunlight made their line look like a huge serpent of blue and steel. The very force of their onset leveled the broad fences bounding the small fields and gardens that interspersed the plain. We could see our shells bursting in their ranks, making great gaps; but on they came, as though they would go straight through and over us. Now we gave them cannister, and that staggered them. A few more paces onward and the Georgians in the road below us rose up, and, glancing an instant along their rifle barrels, let loose a storm of lead into the faces of the advance brigade. This was too much; the column hesitated, and then, turning, took refuge behind the bank. . . .

At 5:30 another attack was made by the enemy, but it was easily repulsed, and the battle of Fredericksburg was over, and Burnside was baffled and defeated.

When the Federals finally withdrew across the Rappahannock River, they had suffered 12,653 casualties, more than double the Rebel losses of 5,309.

~ ~ ~ ~ ~ ~ ~ ~ ~ ~ ~ ~ ~ ~ ~ ~

FROM

The Memoirs of Union Major Frederick Hitchcock

DECEMBER 13, 1862

My brigade had just gone forward in line of battle, and a staff officer directed me to bring the rest of the regiment forward under fire, which I did, fortunately getting them into their proper position. The line was lying prone upon the ground in that open field and trying to maintain a fire against the rebel infantry not more than one hundred and fifty yards in our front behind [a four-foot] stone wall. We were now exposed to the fire of their three lines of infantry, having no shelter whatever. It was like standing upon a raised platform to be shot down by those sheltered behind it. . . . To be sent close up to those lines to maintain a firing-line without any intrenchments or other shelter, was simply to invite wholesale slaughter without the least compensation. It was to attempt the impossible, and invite certain destruction in the effort. . . . [W]e were evidently in a fearful slaughter-pen. Our men were being swept away as by a terrific whirlwind. The ground was soft and spongy from recent rains, and our faces and clothes were bespattered with mud from bullets and fragments of shells striking the ground about us, whilst men were every moment being hit by the storm of projectiles that filled the air. In the midst of that frightful carnage a man rushing by grasped my hand and spoke. I turned and looked into the face of a friend from a distant city. There was a glance of recognition and he was swept away. What his fate was I do not know.

Union general Ambrose Burnside.

Burnside's Fame

While Ambrose Burnside did not make great contributions to the North's military strategy, he is recognized in history for his bushy side whiskers. This dramatic facial hair became known as *sideburns* in honor of General Burnside.

The Battle of Chancellorsville

With 130,000 men to Lee's 75,000, Hooker was in a good position to defeat Lee. The Battle of Chancellorsville was fought in May 1863, very close to the Fredericksburg battlefield. In spite of his advantages, Hooker drew back and allowed Lee to take the initiative. In one of the war's most daring maneuvers, Lee again divided his army; Jackson moved his troops far to the Union right and launched a surprise attack that gave the Confederates another stirring victory.

Before the battle, "Fighting Joe" Hooker had expressed enormous confidence, not only in his army but in himself. "My plans are perfect," he announced before Chancellorsville. "May God have mercy on General Lee for I will have none." After the defeat he said, "I guess I lost confidence in Joe Hooker."

The victory was a costly one for Lee's army: after the battle, Stonewall Jackson and his staff were returning to Lee's camp when Confederate soldiers mistakenly opened fire. Jackson was wounded and died a few days later. Lee had relied heavily on Jackson and this loss forced him to reorganize the Army of Northern Virginia. Some military historians say the army was never again as effective as it had been with Jackson.

The Campaign for Vicksburg

The city of Vicksburg, perched on bluffs high above the Mississippi River, had been turned into a fortress by Confederate engineers. Cannons bristled on the hills overlooking the river. To the north and south, the city was protected by swamps, bayous, and dense thickets. The only way for an army to approach the city was directly from the east through miles of enemy territory.

Over the winter of 1862–1863, Grant's men had tried to dig canals that would place them in an attack position. They also tried to attack through the swamps north of the city, but everything failed. Finally, in April 1863, Grant came up with a brilliant scheme. He would have gunboats and transport barges run the gauntlet of the Vicksburg batteries to a point 30 miles south of the fortress city. Grant's men would march south on the

siege: to surround a city so tightly that no supplies can get in and no humans can get out. One way to beat a siege is to try a "breakout"; another is to have another army attack the force laying the siege.

west bank of the Mississippi and meet the transports, which would then carry them across the mile-wide river. After Grant marched his men for miles and fought several small battles, the Federals finally had the 30,000 defenders of Vicksburg pinned inside their fortifications. When direct assault failed, Grant decided on a **siege**—literally starving the city into surrender. After six weeks of Union bombardment and shrinking food supplies, the 30,000 Confederate troops, and several hundred civilians, could hold out no longer. On July 4, 1863, the Confederate commander at Vicksburg, General John C. Pemberton, surrendered the city and soldiers to General Grant.

In the first reading, Grant's son, Frederick Dent Grant, describes the gunboats and transports in their race past the city. The second selection describes one of the futile attempts to assault the city.

Union gunboats were an important attack weapon for the North, especially on the rivers of the West. These were small paddle-wheel steamboats, often with wood or metal armor plating for protection, and several cannons.

Union gunboats in action on the White River in Arkansas.

FROM

The Memoirs of Brigadier General Frederick Dent Grant

1863

On the 16th of April, 1863, General Grant and Admiral Porter held a final consultation. About 10 P.M. all lights were put out, and the fleet started down the river. Suddenly a rocket went up from the shore; a cannon blazed forth from Warrentown; and a shot passed directly in front of our boat. We stopped; a lurid flame sprang up from a house at De Soto, opposite Vicksburg, then another on the river front, and soon fires were burning along the whole front of the city, and the river was lighted as if by sunlight.

Six gunboats, looking like great black turtles, followed by three fragile transports, moved directly toward the Confederate batteries, which now opened fire. The Benton and the other gunboats responded, and, steaming up near the city, sent shot and shell pouring into Vicksburg. The transports kept over toward the Lousiana shore, and one—the Henry Clay—was set on fire by a red-hot shell, and burned to the water's edge.

The people of Vicksburg lined the hills, and manifested great excitement. On board our boat my father and I stood side by side on the hurricane deck. He was quietly smoking, but an intense light shone in his eyes.

As soon as our fleet passed the batteries, and firing had ceased, father's boat steamed back to Milliken's Bend. The first step of the great campaign had been successfully accomplished.

The Importance of Vicksburg

The Vicksburg victory was enormous for the North. Within a few weeks, the last Rebel defenses on the Mississippi—at Port Hudson—surrendered, and the Union now controlled the entire Mississippi River. And the South lost even more than the North gained: it would be impossible to find 30,000 new recruits; in addition, the mile-wide river now cut the Confederacy in two, isolating Louisiana, Texas, and Arkansas from the other eight states.

ᘓᕀ ᘓᕀ ᘓᕀ ᘓᕀ ᘓᕀ ᘓᕀ ᘓᕀ ᘓᕀ ᘓᕀ ᘓᕀ ᘓᕀ ᘓᕀ ᘓᕀ ᘓᕀ ᘓᕀ

FROM

An Anonymous Account by a Confederate Soldier

MAY 1863

The ditch was passed and the slope gained, but they could go no further. The slope was too steep to be surmounted, and to hold the position was to be fired down upon and exterminated, while the Federal bullets cleared the crest, and dropped to the ground far in the rear. Lighted shells were rolled down the slope and played terrible havoc, and the Federal flags planted in the earth were shot to shreds in less than ten minutes.

Until the recall came they could do nothing but take the steady fire poured down upon them. The wonder is that a single man was left alive. The Regulars lost one third of their total number, and the volunteers suffered such slaughter as few regiments were ever called upon to stand.

During the entire time the Federal troops were in that desperate position they kept banging away at the parapet, but I do not believe that we lost a man killed from their wild firing. The air above us was cut by bullets, and dirt and dust were showered upon us from those striking the parapet, but all the advantage was with us. It was a shameful thing to hold men there as they were held, and it seems a miracle that a single

Plan of the Confederate defenses at Vicksburg. The defenses were built overlooking steep gullies and ravines, making attack almost impossible.

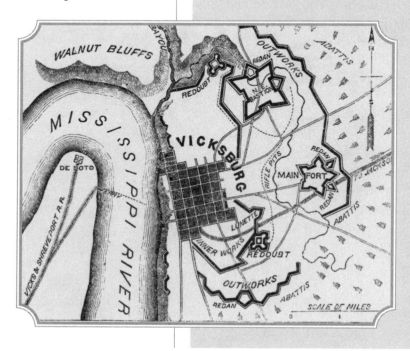

one escaped. The shells made horrible work among them, and after the fight was over and the smoke had blown away, the sight was such that I had never looked upon before or thought possible in war.

"Unconditional Surrender" Grant

Grant's surrender terms, reproduced here, reveal why people said Grant's initials—*U.* and *S.*—stood for "Unconditional Surrender." (He had given similar terms to Forts Henry and Donelson.)

To General Pemberton: Your note of this date is just received, proposing an armistice for several hours, for the purpose of arranging terms of Capitulation through commissioners to be appointed, etc. The useless effusion of blood you propose stopping by this course can be ended at any time you may choose, by the unconditional surrender of the city and the garrison. Men who have shown so much endurance and courage as those now in Vicksburg will always challenge the respect of an adversary, and I can assure you will be treated with all the respect due to prisoners of war. I do not favor the proposition of appointing commissioners to arrange the terms of capitulation, because I have no terms other than those indicated above.

The Battle of Gettysburg

While Grant's army was laying siege to Vicksburg, General Lee launched his well-disguised invasion of Pennsylvania. He had each corps move separately and kept the Blue Ridge Mountains between their march up the Shenandoah Valley and the Union troops east of the mountains. His plan was to attack Harrisburg, the capital of Pennsylvania, and then move against Washington, D.C.

But the plan began to unravel. First, Stuart and his huge cavalry regiment of 10,000 men was to keep an eye on Hooker's Army of the

Potomac, reporting every movement to Lee. But, eager for a little extra glory, Stuart tried to ride completely around the enemy and found himself frequently trapped, forcing him to make an ever-wider circle. The fateful Battle of Gettysburg was nearly over by the time Stuart caught up with Lee.

Without Stuart, Lee learned almost too late that the Army of the Potomac was not only on the move, but was dangerously close to out-flanking Lee's army. He also found out that Hooker had been replaced in command by General George Meade, a much more experienced battlefield leader. Lee suddenly had to prepare for battle long before he was ready.

As it happened, the Union and Confederate forces stumbled into each other on the outskirts of Gettysburg when some Rebels went in search of a shoe factory. The fighting quickly became general. The Yankees were heavily outnumbered and retreated through the town, taking up positions on hills outside Gettysburg. On July 1 and the next day, Lee's forces came very close to smashing through the federal lines, but the Blues somehow managed to hold on as the rest of Meade's army rushed to join them.

In the following reading, a young Union artilleryman, still in his teens, paints a vivid word picture of the head-to-head combat that characterized the first two days of this historic battle.

Union troops defending Little Round Top at the Battle of Gettysburg.

FROM

The Recollections of Augustus Buell

JULY 1, 1863

For seven or eight minutes ensued probably the most desperate fight ever waged between artillery and infantry at close range without a particle of cover on either side. . . .

Up and down the line men reeling and falling, splinters flying from wheels and axles where bullets hit; in the rear, horses tearing and plunging, mad with wounds or terror; drivers yelling, shells bursting, shot shrieking overhead, howling about our ears or throwing up great clouds of dust when they struck; the musketry crashing on three sides of us; bullets hissing, humming and whistling everywhere; cannon roaring; all crash on crash and peal on peal, smoke, dust, splinters, blood, wreck and carnage indescribable; but the brass guns of [our battery] bellowed and not a man flinched or faltered! Every man's shirt soaked with sweat and many of them sopped with blood from wounds not severe enough to make such bulldogs "let go." . . . [And] out in front of us an undulating field, filled almost as far as the eye could reach with a long, low, Confederate gray line creeping toward us, fairly fringed with flame!

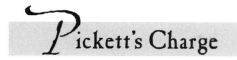

Pickett's Charge

Most students of the Civil War agree that the Battle of Gettysburg was the most dramatic episode of the war—and the most tragic. Everything brave and hopeful that the Confederacy stood for seemed to reach its climax on the battle's third day. In fact, a particular moment in the attack called "Pickett's Charge" is often referred to as the "high-water mark of the Confederacy"—the moment came when some of the Rebels broke through the Yankee lines to the crest of the ridge. In that instant, the

South came as close as it would ever come to winning its independence. But the Confederate wave quickly broke and fell back, starting the final downfall of the Rebel cause.

In the first two days of battle, the Grays had very nearly broken through late on each day, but the Blues rallied just in time. For the third day, Lee ordered a direct attack on the center of the Union line. General James Longstreet, whose corps would make the attack, protested that no charge by 15,000 men could cross a half-mile of open fields against the Union positions on a hill called Cemetery Ridge. But Lee was determined and Longstreet knew he had no choice but to give the order.

The battle began with an artillery bombardment—nearly 150 Confederate cannons hammering at the Union defenses and some 80 federal cannons answering. It was the heaviest bombardment ever heard in North America. An eerie silence followed and then the attack began. The following readings highlight Longstreet's reluctant order to General Pickett and the Rebels' desperate charge across the valley, from Longstreet's own memoirs; and the reactions of Longstreet and Lee to the battle, written by a British observer.

FROM

General James Longstreet's Memoirs

JULY 1863

Picket said, "General, shall I advance?" The effort to speak the order failed, and I could only indicate it by an affirmative bow. He accepted the duty with seeming confidence of success, leaped on his horse, and rode gayly to his command. . . . The officers saluted as they passed, their stern smiles expressing confidence. General Pickett, a graceful horseman, sat lightly in the saddle, his brown locks flowing quite over his shoulders. Pettigrew's division spread their steps and . . . the grand march moved bravely on.

Confederate batteries put their fire over the heads of the men as they moved down the slope, and continued to draw the fire of the enemy until the smoke lifted and drifted to the rear, when every gun was turned upon the infantry columns. . . . Soldiers and officers began to fall, some to rise no more, others to find their way to the hospital tents. Single files were cut here and there, then the gaps increased, and an occasional shot tore wider openings, but, closing the gaps as quickly as made, the march moved on. . . .

Pickett's lines being nearer, the impact was heaviest upon them. Most of the field officers were killed or wounded.

FROM

Arthur J. L. Freemantle's Account

JULY 1863

When I got close up to General Longstreet, I saw one of his regiments advancing through the woods in good order; so, thinking I was just in time to see the attack, I remarked to the General that "I wouldn't have missed this for anything."

Longstreet was seated at the top of a snake fence at the edge of the wood and looked perfectly calm and unperturbed. He replied, laughing: "The Devil you wouldn't! I would like to have missed it very much; we've attacked and been repulsed; look there!"

For the first time I then had a view of the open space between the two positions and saw it covered with Confederates, slowly and sulkily returning toward us in small broken parties, under a heavy fire of artillery. But the fire where we were was not so bad as further to the rear, for although the air seemed alive with shell, yet the greater number burst behind us.

The General told me that Pickett's division had succeeded in carrying the enemy's line and capturing his guns, but after remaining there twenty minutes, it had been forced to retire.

Soon afterward I joined General Lee, who had in the meantime come to the front on becoming aware of the disaster. . . . He was engaged in rallying and in encouraging the broken troops and was riding about a little in front of the wood, quite alone, the whole of his staff being engaged in a similar manner to the rear.

His face, which is always placid and cheerful, did not show any signs of the slightest disappointment, care or annoyance, and he was addressing each soldier he met with a few words of encouragement, such as: "All this will come right in the end; we'll talk it over afterwards; but in the meantime all good men must rally. We want all good men and true just now."

He spoke to all the wounded men that passed him, and the slightly wounded he exhorted to "bind up their hurts and take up a musket" in this emergency. Very few failed to answer his appeal, and I saw many badly wounded men take off their hats and cheer him.

He said to me, "This has been a sad day for us, Colonel—a sad day. But we can't expect always to gain victories."

I saw General Willcox (an officer who wears a short round jacket and a battered straw hat) come up to him and explain, almost crying, the state of his brigade. General Lee immediately shook hands with him and said cheerfully, "Never mind, General, all this has been my fault—it is I that have lost this fight, and you must help me out of it in the best way you can."

The Human Cost of Gettysburg

The casualty count for the three-day battle shocked people throughout America. The Confederates sent 75,000 men into battle; 3,903 were killed, 18,735 were wounded, and 5,425 were missing—this meant 28,063 were casualties, more than one out of every three men. The North numbered 88,289 at the start of the battle. They lost 3,155 dead, 14,529 wounded, and 5,365 missing—a total of 23,049 casualties. No battle in American history, before or since, has taken such a heavy toll.

The Confederate dead at Gettysburg. Camera shutters worked too slowly for action pictures.

COURTESY NATIONAL ARCHIVES

The Aftermath: Southern Gloom, Northern Cheers

As the Battle of Gettysburg ended, the clouds opened up in torrential rains. On July 4, while General Pemberton was surrendering Vicksburg and his army a thousand miles away, Lee's beaten and exhausted troops began their painful withdrawal. The wagonloads of wounded stretched for fourteen miles; the men walking or on horseback dozed as they moved. Finally on July 13, the army crossed the rain-swollen Potomac into Virginia. Lincoln had continually urged Meade to press on and destroy Lee's army before they could cross the river. But the Federals had suffered severely and Meade felt they were in no condition to fight.

People in the North could hardly believe that they had finally beaten Lee's famous Army of Northern Virginia and that this great triumph was combined with Grant's victory at Vicksburg. It seemed impossible for the South to replace the nearly 60,000 men lost in the two battles.

In the first reading, General Josiah Gorgas, in charge of the South's weapons, describes the mood produced by the two defeats; it is followed by a letter written by William Lusk, a Union officer serving in Delaware.

FROM

The Diary of General Josiah Gorgas

JULY 28, 1863

Events have succeeded one another with disastrous rapidity. One brief month ago we were apparently at the point of success. Lee was in Pennsylvania, threatening Harrisburg, and even Philadelphia. Vicksburg seemed to laugh all Grant's efforts to scorn. . . . Now the picture is just as sombre as it was bright then. . . . It seems incredible that human power could effect such a change in so brief a space. Yesterday we rode on the pinnacle of success—today absolute ruin seems to be our portion. The Confederacy totters to its destruction.

FROM

William Lusk's Letter

JULY 7, 1863

Dear, dear Cousin Lou:

I said I would write to you as soon as the full purport of the good news was ascertained. And now that it has all broken upon us, although my heels are where my head ought to be, I will try and fulfill my engagement as coherently as possible. We have had the dark hour. The dawn has broken, and the collapsed confederacy has no place where it can hide its head. Bells are ringing wildly all over the city. Citizens grin at one another with fairly idiotic delight. One is on the top of his house frantically swinging a dinner bell, contributing thus his share of patriotic clamor to the general ding-dong. . . . I can laugh, I can cry with joy. . . . Slavery has fallen, and I believe Heaven as well as earth rejoices. . . . My letter must be short and jubilant, I cannot do anything long today.

Just dance through the house for me, and kiss every one you meet. So I feel now. Good-bye.

Affectionately, Will.

The Gettysburg Address

In the autumn of 1863 ceremonies were held at Gettysburg for the dedication of a national cemetery. President Lincoln addressed the huge gathering, but his address came after the crowd had been listening to Edward Everett, a popular orator, for two hours. Lincoln's speech was so brief that some in the audience did not even realize that he had spoken. Many who did hear it, or read about it in newspapers, were not impressed. Gradually, however, people began to recognize how extraordinary this brief message was. In ten sentences, Lincoln managed to explain the war in terms the people could understand, one of the most eloquent statements in the English language.

Lincoln's Gettysburg Address

NOVEMBER 19, 1863

Four score and seven years ago our fathers brought forth on this continent, a new nation, conceived in liberty, and dedicated to the proposition that all men are created equal.

Now we are engaged in a great civil war, testing whether that nation or any nation so conceived and so dedicated, can long endure. We are met on a great battle-field of that war. We have come to dedicate a portion of that field, as a final resting place for those who gave their lives that that nation might live. It is altogether fitting and proper that we should do this.

But, in a larger sense, we cannot dedicate—we cannot consecrate—we cannot hallow—this ground. The brave men, living and dead, who struggled here, have consecrated it, far above our poor power to add or detract. The world will little note, nor long remember what we say here, but it can never forget what they did here. It is for us the living, rather, to be dedicated here to the unfinished work which they who fought here have thus far so nobly advanced. It is rather for us to be here dedicated to the great task remaining before us—that from these honored dead we take increased devotion to that cause for which they gave the last full measure of devotion—that we here highly resolve that these dead shall not have died in vain—that this nation, under God, shall have a new birth of freedom—and that government of the people, by the people, for the people, shall not perish from the earth.

Hospitals and Medical Care

In many ways, the Civil War was the first modern war—a war fought with rifles that could shoot farther and faster than any previous weapon; artillery that included exploding shells and incendiary (fire-producing) shells that could hit a target up to five miles away; and armies, which had once numbered 10,000 to 20,000 men, that now numbered 130,000 or more.

What was not new, however, was treatment for the sick and wounded. Doctors used methods and equipment that were more suitable to the 1700s than to the mid-1800s. Physicians knew nothing about antiseptics;

wounds were probed with bare unwashed fingers; amputations were made with knives and bone saws that had not been cleaned; and wounds were sewn up with needles and threads taken from the supply that dangled from buttonholes in the surgeon's blood-spattered coat.

The following reading will give you some of the grim details of medical care, but it also shows the compassion and dedication of doctors and nurses. The selection is from the diary of Louisa May Alcott, later the author of *Little Women* (1868), who was a nurse during the war and later wrote about the experience in a book called *Hospital Sketches*.

A Union field hospital in Virginia.

FROM

The Diary of Louisa May Alcott

JANUARY 4, 1863

Up at six, dress by gas light, run through my ward & fling up the windows though the men grumble & shiver; but the air is bad enough to breed a **pestilence** & as no notice is taken of our frequent appeals for better ventilation I must do what I can do. Poke up the fire, add blankets, joke, coax & command, but continue to open doors and windows as if life depended on it; mine does, & doubtless many another, for a more perfect pestilence box than this house I never saw—cold, damp, dirty, full of vile odors from wounds, kitchen, wash rooms, and stables. No competent head, male or female, to right matters, & a jumble of good, bad, & indifferent nurses, surgeons, and attendants to complicate the Chaos still more.

pestilence: disease.

> After this unwelcome progress through my stifling ward I go to breakfast with what appetite I may; find the inevitable fried beef, salt butter, husky bread, and washy coffee. . . . Till noon I trot, trot, giving out rations, cutting up food for helpless "boys," washing faces, teaching my attendants how beds are made or floors swept, dressing wounds, taking Dr. FitsPatrick's orders (privately wishing all the time that he would be more gentle with my big babies), dusting tables, sewing bandages, keeping my tray tidy, rushing up and down after pillows, bed linen, sponges, book and directions, till it seems as if I would joyfully pay down all I possess for fifteen minutes' rest.

The Tragedy of Timing

In France, during the mid-1860s, Dr. Louis Pasteur was finishing his experiments proving that germs cause disease. At nearly the same time, Dr. Joseph Lister in Scotland was showing that using antiseptic solutions to sterilize medical intruments and to keep wounds clean had a miraculous effect on reducing infections. Between 1865 and 1870, Lister combined his methods with Pasteur's theories in his hospital. In the past, 50 percent of patients with amputations had died—about the same as in American military hospitals. By 1870, Lister had reduced the death rate to 15 percent. If the timing had been different, the work of Lister and Pasteur might have changed some of the horrors of Civil War battlefields.

Clara Barton: Angel of the Battlefield

After witnessing the suffering of the wounded after the first battle of Bull Run, Clara Barton, a forty-year-old clerk in the Washington, D.C., Patent Office, decided she had to become involved. She placed an ad in her hometown (Worcester, Massachusetts) newspaper asking for medicines, food, blankets, and cotton for bandages. Supplies poured in and Clara Barton had found a new career.

She wanted to help on the scene as much as possible and became the first woman allowed at the battlefield by Union army generals. Her help for the wounded and sick led the soldiers to call her the "Angel of the Battlefield." But Barton's greatest contribution was getting things done. She generally worked alone, with no official connection to the army or to the Sanitary Commission, an organization that established field hospitals. Almost single-handedly, she organized a bureau for locating missing soldiers and for marking the graves of those who had died. After the war, she worked on the battlefields of Europe and then became the major force in creating the American Red Cross, serving as its director for more than twenty years.

The following selection, from Clara Barton's war diary, describes her actions when she found that wounded Union soldiers were not being cared for. The incident took place in 1864 at Fredericksburg, Virginia.

Clara Barton.

ಜಿ ಜಿ ಜಿ ಜಿ ಜಿ ಜಿ ಜಿ ಜಿ ಜಿ ಜಿ ಜಿ ಜಿ ಜಿ ಜಿ ಜಿ

FROM

Clara Barton's War Diary

1864

I saw, crowded into one old sunken hotel, lying helpless upon its bare, wet, bloody floors, five hundred fainting men hold up their cold, bloodless, dingy hands, as I passed, and beg me in Heaven's name for a cracker to keep them from starving (and I had none). . . . I saw two hundred six-mule army wagons in a line, ranged down the street . . . and reaching so far out on the Wilderness road that I never found the end of it; every wagon crowded with wounded men, stopped, standing in the rain and mud . . . all night and how much longer I know not. The dark spot in the mud under many a wagon, told only too plainly where some poor fellow's life had dripped out in those dreadful hours.

I remembered one man who would set it right, if he knew of it, who possessed the power and who would believe me. . . . With difficulty, I obtained . . . four stout horses with a light army wagon [which] took me ten miles at an unbroken gallop, through field and swamp and stumps and mud to Belle Plain and a steam tug at once to Washington. Landing at dusk I sent for Henry Wilson, chairman of the Military Committee of the Senate. A messenger brought him at eight. . . . At ten he stood in the War Department and [managed to convince them]. . . .

At two o'clock in the morning the Quartermaster-General and staff galloped to the 6th Street wharf; at ten they were in Fredericksburg. At noon the wounded men were fed from the food of the city and the houses were opened to the [men] of the Union Army. . . . In three days I returned with carloads of supplies.

Prison Hell: Escape from Andersonville

Prison camps were miserable places throughout the war, but after 1863, the suffering became even worse. Andersonville, a Confederate prison in southern Georgia, was designed to hold 10,000 for short periods; by early 1864, it held 24,000 Union troops and the South had no way of feeding or providing medical help for that many. Hundreds died every day from starvation or disease. John L. Ransom, close to death from scurvy and starvation, still kept his diary, ending up with four volumes in all. After getting out of Andersonville with the help of his Indian friend Battese— as described in the following excerpt—he spent three months in a

Confederate hospital. Partially recovered, he was put on a prison train for Florida; he escaped, was recaptured, escaped again, and finally, in December, made his way to Sherman's Union army in Georgia.

Andersonville Prison in Georgia.

Ϡϝ Ϡϝ Ϡϝ Ϡϝ Ϡϝ Ϡϝ Ϡϝ Ϡϝ Ϡϝ Ϡϝ Ϡϝ Ϡϝ Ϡϝ Ϡϝ

FROM

John L. Ransom's Diary

1 8 6 4

July 27

Sweltering hot. No worse than yesterday. Said that two hundred die now each day. Rowe very bad and Sanders getting so. Swan dead, Gordon dead, Jack Withers dead, Scotty dead, a large Irishman who has been near us a long time, is dead.

These and scores of others died yesterday and day before.

Hub Dakin came to see me, and brought an onion. He is just able to crawl around himself.

One reason for the horrifying prison conditions was that General Grant ordered an end to prisoner exchanges. Until 1864, it had been common for generals to arrange an exchange of prisoners with the enemy's commander. This eased the burden on the inadequate prison facilities. Grant changed the policy because he realized that the exchanges allowed the Rebels to rebuild their manpower. While this decision fit Grant's plan of weakening the enemy, it also added to the suffering and death in the camps.

July 28

Taken a step toward the [burial] trenches since yesterday, and am worse. Had a wash all over this morning. Battese took me to the creek; carried me without any trouble.

July 29

Alive and kicking. Drank some soured water made from meal and water.

July 30

Hang on well, and no worse.

Marine Hospital, Savannah, GA, September 15

A great change has taken place since I last wrote in my diary. Am in heaven now, compared with the past. At about midnight, September 7th, our detachment was ordered outside at Andersonville, and Battese picked me up and carried me to the gate.

The men were being let outside in ranks of four, and counted as they went out. They were very strict about letting none go but the well ones, or those who could walk. The Rebel Adjutant stood upon a box by the gate, watching very close. Pitch-pine knots were burning in the near vicinity to give light.

As it came our turn to go, Battese got me in the middle of the rank, stood me up as well as I could stand, and with himself on one side and Sergeant Rowe on the other, began pushing our way through the gate. Could not help myself a particle, and was so faint that I hardly knew what was going on.

As we were going through the gate the Adjutant yelled out: "Here, here! Hold on there, that man can't go, hold on there!"

And Battese crowding right along outside. The Adjutant struck over the heads of the men and tried to stop us, but my noble Indian friend kept straight ahead, hallooing: "He all right, he well, he go!"

And so I got outside, the Adjutant having too much to look after to follow me. After we were outside, I was carried to the railroad.

PART VI

THE FALL OF THE CONFEDERACY

After the Union victories at Vicksburg and Gettysburg, the hopes of the Confederacy seemed pretty well ruined. Lee's army scarcely looked like an army as the men trooped back to Virginia, their uniforms in tatters, many of the men shoeless. To make matters worse, a Union army in the West, led by Ulysses S. Grant, won another brilliant victory, this time in the Battle of Chattanooga late in 1863. That triumph convinced Lincoln to promote Grant to command all the Union armies.

The South, however, was not ready to give up. Somehow, Lee patched together his Army of Northern Virginia and prepared to defend Richmond. In the West, Joe Johnston still commanded a tough army of 65,000 veterans ready to defend Atlanta, Georgia. Grant left his trusted assistant, General William Tecumseh Sherman, to face Johnston while Grant himself went to Washington to take overall command and to advance with Meade's Army of the Potomac.

The war now entered its final year. It was to be the grimmest year—and the costliest in terms of deaths and destruction. The readings in part VI offer a survey of the war's final chapter.

Grant, Sherman, and Total War

Union general William Tecumseh Sherman.

Generals Grant and Sherman brought a new approach to war. Their goal was not only to defeat the opposing army, but also to destroy the enemy's will and ability to continue fighting. Destroying a region's crops and warehouses, for example, depleted an army's supplies and fighting on short rations took a heavy toll.

After 1900, this approach became known as "total war," involving the entire society in a war effort that could eventually touch the lives of every individual in the warring nations.

In May 1864, while Sherman led his Army of Tennessee into Georgia, Grant began his relentless drive against Lee and Richmond in the East. During May and June, the Army of the Potomac, numbering 122,000 men, hammered at Lee's 60,000-man Army of Northern Virginia. In the most gruesome fighting of the war, Lee steadily retreated but his ragged troops repeatedly blunted Grant's efforts to corner them and force a surrender.

Grant in Washington

When Grant arrived in Washington early in 1864, he was treated as a great hero. Crowds in the White House were so huge that he had to stand on a sofa to avoid the crush. In his faded private's uniform, and with his hair and beard in their characteristically scruffy state, he presented a strange contrast to sophisticated West Pointers like McClellan and Grant's other predecessors. Some said he looked like a tough "Westerner" who knew how to fight. Others were not so sure. "He hasn't faced Bobby Lee yet," they said.

The following selections, both by men in Grant's army, provide a sampling of the grim warfare produced by their commander's tactics. The battles described are the Wilderness and Spotsylvania.

FROM

The Memoirs of Private Warren Goss

MAY 1864

[The Wilderness was a densely forested area, where the men continually tripped over skulls and bones, grim reminders of a Rebel victory there a year earlier.]

The scene of savage fighting with the ambushed enemy, which followed, defies description. No one could see the fight fifty feet from him. The roll and crackle of the musketry was something terrible, even to the veterans of many battles. The lines were very near each other, and from the dense underbrush and the tops of the trees came puffs of smoke, the "ping" of the bullets, and the yell of the enemy. It was a blind and bloody hunt to the death, in bewildering thickets, rather than a battle.

Amid the tangled, darkened woods, the *"ping! ping! ping!"* the *"pop! pop! pop!"* of the rifles, and the long roll and roar of musketry blending on our right and left, were terrible. In advancing it was next to impossible to preserve a distinct line, and we were constantly broken into small groups. The underbrush scratched our faces, tore our clothing and tripped our feet from under us constantly. . . .

Flames sprang up in the woods in our front, where the fight of the morning had taken place. With crackling roar, like an army of fire, it came down upon the Union line. The wind drove the blinding smoke and suffocating heat into our faces. This, added to the oppressive heat of the weather,

The Death of "Jeb" Stuart

A few miles from Spotsylvania, at the village of Yellow Tavern, Stuart was shot while his cavalry was defending the road to Richmond. Thrown from his horse, he tried to escape on foot but was quickly shot down. Lee said, "I can hardly think of him without weeping."

was almost unendurable. It soon became terrible. The line of fire, with resistless march, swept the thickets before its advance, then reaching out its tongue of flame, ignited the breastworks composed of resinous logs, which soon roared and crackled along their entire length. The men fought the enemy and the flames at the same time. Their hair and beards were singed and their faces blistered. . . .

During the conflict our men had exhausted their ammunition and had been obliged to gather cartridges from the dead and wounded. Their rifles, in many instances, became so hot by constant firing, that they were unable to hold them in their hands. The fire was the most terrible enemy our men met that day, and few survivors will forget this attack of the flames on their lines.

FROM

The Memoirs of Horace Porter

MAY 1864

[After the Battle of the Wilderness, Grant thought he would go around Lee's flank and race for the crossroads called Spotsylvania. But Lee guessed Grant's plan and had his men in position when the startled Federals reached the crossroads.]

It was chiefly a savage hand-to-hand fight across the breastworks. Rank after rank was riddled by shot and shell and bayonet thrusts, and finally sank, a mass of torn and mutilated corpses; then fresh troops rushed madly forward to replace the dead; and so the murderous work went on. . . . Muskets were fired with muzzle against muzzle. Skulls were crushed with clubbed muskets and men stabbed with swords and bayonets thrust between the logs in the parapet which separated the combatants. Wild cheers, savage yells, and frantic shrieks rose above the sighing of the wind and the pattering of rain and formed a demonical accompaniment to the booming of the guns.

A field sketch of federal and Confederate positions during the Battle of Spotsylvania. The cartographer, Jed Hotchkiss, was one of the most skilled mapmakers. In this sketch, he included the names of Confederate commanders, like Stuart and Early.

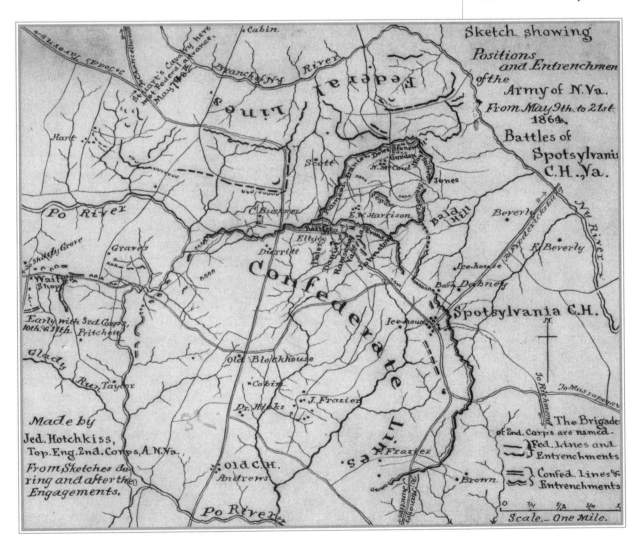

Assessing Grant's Tactics

In one month of fighting (early May to early June 1864), the Union losses had been incredible: 55,000 men killed, wounded, or missing. That was more than 41 percent of the men Grant had started with—all for a gain of 70 miles. The South's losses were also heavy. In fact the Confederacy suffered 32,000 casualties—including 22 of their 58 generals—about 46 percent of Lee's original force.

In spite of the dismay over the casualty figures, Northerners could see that Grant's strategy was working. By late June, the gaps in Grant's divisions had been filled with new recruits. Lee, on the other hand, could not bring in enough men to bring his army back up to strength. It was only a matter of time before the Rebels would be hopelessly outnumbered.

Sherman's Campaign in Georgia

Confederate General John B. Hood

General Hood, who replaced Johnston as the Federals closed in on Atlanta, was one of the bravest men in either army. He lost the use of one arm at Gettysburg, then had a leg amputated at the Battle of Chickamauga. He continued to lead his men into battle while strapped to his saddle.

Although Grant's relentless drive against Lee was slowly grinding down Southern resistance, the casualty toll was destroying morale in the North. By August, Lincoln was convinced that he could not win reelection, especially against the Democrats' peace candidate, the popular General George McClellan.

Grant realized he had to modify his strategy. He bypassed Richmond and attacked Petersburg, a rail center twenty miles away. And, instead of direct attacks, he used siege tactics as he had done at Vicksburg. The siege of Petersburg, however, was destined to last for ten months.

Meantime, in the West, Sherman moved into Georgia, pitting his army of 110,000 against a Rebel force of 60,000 under General Joe Johnston. Johnston's stubborn defense slowed Sherman's advance to a crawl from May 1864 to August. Then President Jefferson Davis stepped in. Frustrated that Johnston did not attack, he replaced him with General John Hood.

Hood made the mistake of trying to attack Sherman's army and, within days, was forced to abandon Atlanta. On September 2, 1864, Sherman telegraphed Lincoln: "So Atlanta is ours and fairly won!"

Atlanta was a resounding victory for Sherman and for the Union. Suddenly, Lincoln's reelection was assured and he easily beat McClellan in November.

A cartoon poking fun at General George B. McClellan in his campaign for the presidency in 1864. The candidate is firmly in his saddle, but the saddle is mounted safely on a gunboat in the James River, while his army is losing to the Confederates near Richmond in 1862. The name of the gunboat is the hometown of General Ulysses S. Grant.

When Sherman asked permission to march from Atlanta to the Atlantic coast, Lincoln and Grant agreed. "I can make the march," Sherman promised, "and make Georgia howl!" With 62,000 men (leaving another 60,000 to take care of Hood's army), Sherman had his men cut a swath sixty miles wide across Georgia, destroying everything in their path that could help the South continue fighting. Special units, called Sherman's "Bummers," went beyond the general's orders and seized everything of value, including jewelry, silverware, furniture, and clothing. The following reading presents a young Georgian's reaction.

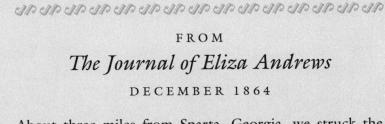

FROM

The Journal of Eliza Andrews

DECEMBER 1864

About three miles from Sparta, Georgia, we struck the "burnt country," as it is so well named by the natives. . . . I almost felt as if I should like to hang a Yankee myself. There

"War Is Hell"

General Sherman has long been known for the blunt statement "War is Hell!" But he actually said this in a speech some years after the war. During the war, when Atlanta citizens protested his decision to evacuate all civilians, he said, "War is cruelty and you cannot refine it! You might as well appeal against the thunderstorm as against these terrible hardships of war."

was hardly a fence left standing all the way from Sparta to Gordon. The fields were trampled down and the road was lined with carcasses of horses, hogs and cattle that the invaders, unable either to consume or carry away with them, had wantonly shot down, to starve out the people and prevent them from making their crops. The stench in some places was unbearable. . . . The dwellings that were standing all showed signs of pillage. . . . here and there lone chimney stacks, "Sherman's sentinels," told of homes lain in ashes. The infamous wretches! I couldn't wonder now that those poor people should want to put a rope around the neck of every red-handed devil of 'em.

Destruction at Charleston, South Carolina, by Sherman's army late in the war.

COURTESY NATIONAL ARCHIVES

Surrender at Appomattox

Sherman's destructive march through Georgia reached the Atlantic coast in December 1864 and Sherman's wire to Lincoln offered him the city of Savannah as a Christmas present. Sherman's boisterous troops now turned north to connect with Grant at Petersburg. As they entered South Carolina, the Union army began to inflict even greater damage, because that state had started the secession movement.

Lee could see that his tattered army, now reduced to less than 30,000 half-starved men, would soon be trapped between two powerful armies. The readings in this section cover the last days of the Confederacy. First, General Grant describes his meeting with Lee at Appomattox; then Mary Boykin Chesnut describes how some of the elite families of the Confederacy received the news of surrender.

FROM
General Grant's Memoirs
APRIL 9, 1865

We greeted each other, and after shaking hands took our seats. I had my staff with me, a good portion of whom were in the room during the whole of the interview.

What General Lee's feelings were I do not know. As he was a man of much dignity, with an impassible face, it was impossible to say whether he felt inwardly glad that the end had finally come, or felt sad over the result, and was too manly to show it. Whatever his feelings, they were entirely concealed from my observation; but my own feelings, which had been quite jubilant on the receipt of his letter, were sad and depressed. I felt like anything rather than rejoicing at the downfall of a foe who had fought so long and valiantly, and had suffered so much for a cause, though that cause was, I believe, one of the worst for which a people ever fought, and one for which there was the least excuse. I do not question, however, the sincerity of the great mass of those who were opposed to us.

General Lee was dressed in a full uniform which was entirely new, and was wearing a sword of considerable value, very likely the sword which had been presented by the State of Virginia; at all events, it was an entirely different sword from the one that would ordinarily be worn in the field. In my rough traveling suit, the uniform of a private with the straps of a lieutenant-general, I must have contrasted very strangely with a man so handsomely dressed, six feet high and of faultless form. But this was not a matter that I thought of until afterwards. . . .

[At Lee's request, Grant wrote terms of surrender.]

General Lee, after all was completed and before taking his leave, remarked that his army was in a very bad condition for want of food, and that they were without forage; that his men had been living for some days on parched corn exclusively, and that he would have to ask me for rations and forage. I told him "certainly," and asked for how many men he wanted rations. His answer was "about twenty-five thousand": and I authorized him to send his own commissary and quartermaster to Appomattox Station.

When news of the surrender first reached our lines our men commenced firing a salute of a hundred guns in honor of the victory. I at once sent word, however, to have it stopped. The Confederates were now our prisoners, and we did not want to exult over their downfall.

The Final Chapter for Jefferson Davis

Until the very end of the war, Davis insisted the North would soon tire of Confederate resistance and ask for peace. As federal troops moved in, Davis tried to flee. He was quickly captured, charged with treason, and imprisoned at Fort Monroe, Virginia. He was never put on trial; instead, he was quietly released in May 1867. He and his wife settled on a Mississippi plantation, where he wrote his own account of the Confederacy. The political leaders of Mississippi wanted to send him to the U.S. Senate—a typical act of loyalty in the states of the former Confederacy. Davis, however, proudly refused to ask for a pardon that would have allowed him to be a senator.

Poor Major McLean

In 1861, Major William McLean owned a handsome estate in Virginia called Yorkshire. It became the headquarters for the Confederates during the first Battle of Bull Run (or Manassas). The house and grounds were used to house several regiments; at one point, a cannon shell clattered down the chimney and exploded in a kettle of stew cooking in the fireplace.

As soon as he could, McLean moved his family farther south, far from the sound of battle. Unfortunately, the village he chose was Appomattox Courthouse. And, of course, it was the McLean House that was chosen for the Lee-Grant surrender negotiations. Afterward, every officer wanted a souvenir of the historic meeting and the house was rapidly stripped of its furniture.

The McLean House at Appomattox Courthouse, Virginia, where Lee surrendered to Grant in April 1865.

LIBRARY OF CONGRESS

FROM

Mary Boykin Chesnut's Diary

APRIL 19, 1865

Just now, when Mr. Clay dashed up-stairs, pale as a sheet, saying, "General Lee has capitulated," I saw it reflected in Mary Darby's face before I heard him speak. She staggered to the table, sat down, and wept aloud. Mr. Clay's eyes were not dry. Quite beside herself Mary shrieked, "Now we belong to negroes and Yankees!" Buck [Sally Buchanan Preston, Mrs. Chesnut's close friend] said, "I do not believe it."

While the Preston girls are here, my dining-room is given up to them, and we camp on the landing, with our one table and six chairs. Beds are made on the dining-room

The Final Tragedy

By April 10, 1865, it seemed that the American people had suffered as much as they could bear. Then came the news that President Lincoln had been mortally wounded on April 14 by assassin John Wilkes Booth at Fords Theater in Washington. He died the next day. Secretary of State Seward was stabbed but survived.

The celebrations of victory and reunion suddenly had a pall of sadness cast over them. As one Northern newspaper put it, "The songs of victory are drowned in sorrow."

floor. Otherwise there is no furniture except buckets of water and bath-tubs in their improvised chamber. Night and day this landing and these steps are crowded with the *elite* of the Confederacy, going and coming, and when night comes, or rather, bedtime, more beds are made on the floor of the landing-place for the war-worn soldiers to rest upon.

My husband is rarely at home. I sleep with the girls, and my room is given up to soldiers. General Lee's few, but undismayed, his remnant of an army, or the part of it from the South and West, sad and crestfallen, pass through Chester. Many discomfited heroes find their way up these stairs.

We are to stay here. Running is useless now; so we mean to bide a Yankee raid, which they say is imminent. Why fly? They are everywhere, these Yankees, like red ants, like the locusts and frogs which were the plagues of Egypt.

The plucky way in which our men keep up is beyond praise. There is no howling, and our poverty is made a matter of laughing. We deride our own penury. Of the country we try not to speak at all.

Mary Boykin Chesnut

Mary Chesnut wrote one of the greatest diaries of the Civil War, a detailed, day-by-day account filled with humor and insight. She had the advantage of being married to James Chesnut, a former senator, who served on President Jefferson Davis's staff, providing her with information about practically all the leading men and women of the Confederacy. She was also a puzzle to many of her Southern friends because of her attitudes toward slavery. Her husband's family owned hundreds of slaves, but she hated slavery and openly declared it would end no matter which side won the war. In addition, Mary Chesnut was an outspoken champion of women's rights, an unusual position for a Southern woman. She reworked her diaries after the war, but they were not published until 1905, twenty years after her death.

PART VII

RESTORING THE UNION

Any war is followed by a time of difficult, painful adjustments. For the American people in 1865, the adjustments were made even more difficult by the terrible losses suffered by both sides, as well as by the death of Lincoln, the one person who could have helped heal some of the deepest wounds.

With Lincoln gone, a powerful group of Senate Repubicans put forward their plan for *Reconstruction* (the process of bringing the eleven states of the former Confederacy back into the United States). They divided the eleven states of the former Confederacy into five military districts, with an army general in command of each. Instead of Lincoln's idea of a lenient policy for restoring the states to the Union, these "Radical Republicans" were treating them like conquered territory. When President Andrew Johnson, Lincoln's successor, tried to block the Radicals' plans, the Senate *impeached* him (charged him with acts that would lead to his removal from office). The specific charge

121

was that Johnson had violated a federal law by removing officials without the consent of the Senate.

For several weeks in early 1868, the nation experienced its first presidential impeachment trial, with the Senate sitting as the jury. A two-thirds vote of the senators was needed for a guilty verdict, and Johnson was acquitted by a single vote.

Over the next four years, the Republicans' plan for Reconstruction gradually restored the eleven states to the Union. The readings in part VII will provide evidence of the successes and failures of Reconstruction.

New Rights for African Americans

Blacks in Politics

With the help of the Freedmen's Bureau, thousands of adult African American men registered to vote. An estimated 500,000 were registered in time to help Ulysses S. Grant become president in 1868. Some blacks also became active in politics. Between 1868 and 1876, fourteen blacks served in the House of Representatives and two in the Senate. They were even more numerous in state and local governments.

While some Radical Republicans wanted to punish the South for the war, others had a sincere desire to help the country's four million freed slaves gain their rightful place in a democratic society. One important step was the creation of a Freedmen's Bureau to help the former slaves adjust to their new lives. The bureau's greatest success was in establishing several colleges and more than four thousand schools in the South.

The first African American senator and members of the House of Representatives. Senator Hiram R. Revels, on the left, served from 1870 to 1871; ironically, he completed the unfinished term of Jefferson Davis, elected in 1864.

LIBRARY OF CONGRESS

In the following selection, Booker T. Washington, who became one of the first great African American leaders, tells how his journey to gain an education began.

The Thirteenth Amendment to the Constitution, ratified in 1865, marked the official end of slavery. The next two amendments were designed to protect the rights of African Americans. The Fourteenth Amendment (1868) guaranteed all citizens equal protection of the laws. The Fifteenth Amendment stated that the right to vote could not be denied "on account of race, color, or previous condition of servitude [slavery]."

FROM

Booker T. Washington's Up from Slavery

1872

One day, while at work in the coal-mine, I happened to overhear two miners talking about a great school for coloured people somewhere in Virginia. This was the first time that I had ever heard anything about any kind of school or college that was more pretentious than the little coloured school in our town.

In the darkness of the mine I noiselessly crept as close as I could to the two men who were talking. I heard one tell the other that not only was the school established for the members of my race, but that opportunities were provided by which poor but worthy students could work out all or a part of the cost of board, and at the same time be taught some trade or industry.

As they went on describing the school, it seemed to me that it must be the greatest place on earth, and not even Heaven presented more attractions for me at that time than did the Hampton Normal and Agricultural Institute in Virginia about which these men were talking. I resolved at once to go to that school, although I had no idea where it was, or how many miles away, or how I was going to reach it; I remembered only that I was on fire constantly with one ambition, and that was to go to Hampton. This thought was with me day and night. . . .

Life at Hampton was a constant revelation to me; was

White Backlash

Southern whites, especially Confederate veterans, hated the Reconstruction policies of the Radical Republicans. Some reacted by forming secret societies to oppose Republican rule and to undermine the rights of African Americans. Members of the most notorious group—the Ku Klux Klan, or KKK—dressed in white robes and hoods to give the appearance of being the ghosts of Confederate soldiers. Riding in bands of fifty or more, they intimidated blacks, dragging them from their homes to frighten them and sometimes to administer beatings or whippings. At times, they even resorted to lynching (executing without a trial, usually by hanging).

constantly taking me into a new world. The matter of having meals at regular hours, of eating on a tablecloth, using a napkin, the use of the bath-tub and of the toothbrush, as well as the use of sheets upon the bed, were all new to me.

Carpetbaggers and Scalawags

Thousands of Northerners moved to the South after the war. Many were teachers, including hundreds of women, while others came to start businesses or to invest in railroads. Southern whites called these visitors "carpetbaggers"—people who came to fill their carpetbags (suitcases) with Southern money. Some carpetbaggers were guilty of illegal schemes, but most came with honest intentions and helped to rebuild the South's economy.

Even more despised were the "scalawags"—a name given to Southern whites who had remained loyal to the Union. Many scalawags were poor or middle-class whites who had opposed the plantation system and slavery.

Restoring Southern Control in the South

Reconstruction gradually came to an end in the 1870s. One reason for the change was that Northerners lost interest in maintaining control of the South. Then, in 1872, Congress passed an Amnesty Act, restoring the rights of Confederate veterans, except for those who had been the top military and political leaders. This helped to strengthen the Democratic Party and its opposition to Republican rule. By 1875, the Democrats controlled eight of the eleven states of the former Confederacy.

The strength of the Democratic Party was increased by public outrage over political corruption at all levels of government throughout the postwar years. Much of the corruption was blamed on the Republicans, including members of Congress and the administration of President Grant.

In 1876, Americans were beginning to prepare for a great centennial celebration to mark the nation's one hundredth birthday. Workers were constructing dozens of new buildings in Philadelphia to house a huge Centennial Exposition. *Scribner's Monthly* magazine used the occasion to express hope that America would truly be reunited. Portions of the editorial are included in the selection that follows.

The 1876 Election

In the 1876 presidential election, the Democrats nominated New York governor Samuel Tilden with the campaign slogan of "Tilden and Reform." When the votes were counted, Tilden seemed to have won over Rutherford B. Hayes, governor of Ohio and a former Union army general. Tilden, however, had only 184 electoral votes and he needed 185 to be elected; but the electoral votes from Florida, Louisiana, and South Carolina, plus one vote from Oregon, were disputed—a total of 20 votes. Congress created a special Electoral Commission to resolve the dispute. The commission awarded all twenty votes to Hayes, giving him the presidency by a vote of 185 to 184.

Many Southern Democrats were outraged by what they called "the Stolen Election," and there was some fear that the Civil War could be resumed. But even before his election, Hayes had promised that he would remove all remaining federal troops from the South and make funds available for building railroads in the region to help strengthen the economy. Hayes kept his promises and his inauguration in March 1877 is considered the official end of Reconstruction.

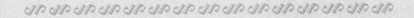

FROM

Scribner's Monthly

AUGUST 1875

We are to have grand doings next year. . . . The Centennial is expected to celebrate in a fitting way the birth of a nation.

The great point is to recognize the fact that . . . these United States constitute a nation; that we are to live, grow, prosper, and suffer together, united by bands that cannot be sundered. Unless this fact is fully recognized throughout the Union, our Centennial will be but a hollow mockery.

A few weeks ago, Mr. Jefferson Davis, the ex-president of the Confederacy, was reported to have urged an audience to be as loyal to the old flag of the Union now as they were during the Mexican War. If the South could know what music there was in these words to the northern ears. . . .

People of the South, we want you. We would see . . . all causes and all memories of discord wiped out forever. You do not believe this? Then you do not know the heart of the North. Have you cause of complaint against the politicians? Alas! So have we. Help us loving and loyal American citizens, to make our politicians better. There is nothing that the North wants so much today, as that the old relations between you and us are forever restored—that your hope, your pride, and your destiny are one with ours.

Ulysses S. Grant's Last Battle

After his great success in leading the Union to victory, General Grant was rewarded by being elected president in 1868 and reelected in 1872. He enjoyed most of his time in the White House, but he was not a good president, at least in terms of the men he surrounded himself with. By the middle of his second term it became clear that members of his administration had been engaged in numerous schemes to defraud the government. Although none of the scandals involved Grant directly, his presidency was remembered as the most corrupt up to that point in the nation's history.

Within a few years of leaving office, Grant was defrauded by his business associates. Now penniless, he received yet another blow when he learned that he was dying of throat cancer, brought on by years of heavy cigar smoking. Determined not to leave his family penniless, Grant spent his last years writing his memoirs, dictating the last few pages just before he died. His friend, the famed author and humorist Mark Twain, helped publish the two volumes, which are still regarded as outstanding military history. The memoirs provided his wife and family with a good-sized fortune.

SOURCES

PART I North and South Drift Apart

Solomon Northrup, *Twelve Years a Slave,* 1853: from William Loren Katz, ed., *Eyewitness: The Negro in American History* (Belmont, Calif.: David S. Lake Publisher, 1974), pp. 188f.

Theodore Weld, *American Slavery As It Is: The Testimony of a Thousand Witnesses,* 1839: from Ralph K. Andrist, ed., *The American Heritage History of the Making of the Nation* (New York: American Heritage Publishing Co., 1968), pp. 325–326.

Lowell Offering, c. 1843: adapted from Benita Eisler, ed., *The Lowell Offerings: Writings by New England Mill Women (1840–1845)* (New York: Harper & Row Publishers, 1977), pp. 136–137.

Richmond Enquirer, "24th August, 1831, 3 O'clock": from David Davis and Steven Mintz, eds., *The Boisterous Sea of Liberty: A Documentary History of America from Discovery through the Civil War* (New York: Oxford University Press, 1998), pp.387–388.

Liberator, September 3, 1831: from Davis and Mintz, *The Boisterous Sea,* p. 390.

Kale's Letter to John Quincy Adams, January 4, 1841: from Simon Baldwin, "The Captives of the *Amistad,*" *Papers of the New Haven Historical Society,* vol. 4 (1888), pp. 354–355; excerpted in *The Boisterous Sea,* pp. 424–425.

PART II The Deepening Crisis

Senator Henry Clay's Compromise Speech, February 5, 1850: from the *Congressional Globe, Appendix,* p. 315, reprinted in Robert C. Cotner et al., *Readings in American History,* vol. 1, 1492 to 1865 (Boston: Houghton Mifflin, 1976), pp. 298f.

Senator John C. Calhoun's Answer for the South, March 4, 1850: from Cotner et al., *Readings,* pp. 305f.

Senator Daniel Webster's Speech for Compromise, March 7, 1850: from Cotner et al., *Readings,* pp. 308f.

A Speech by Frederick Douglass, August 1852: from the Frederick Douglass Papers, in Milton Meltzer, ed., *Voices from the Civil War* (New York: Thomas Y. Crowell Publishers, 1989), pp. 12f.

Charles E. Stevens's Eyewitness Account, June 1854: from Charles E. Stevens, *Anthony Burns: A History;* excerpts in Paul Angle, ed., *The American Reader* (New York: Rand McNally Corp., 1956), pp. 289–291.

Levi Coffin's Recollections, c. 1850: from *The Reminiscences of Levi Coffin, 1876,* excerpted in David Colbert, ed., *Eyewitness to America* (New York: Random House, 1997), pp. 182f.

Henry "Box" Brown's Account, c. 1852: from John F. Bayliss, ed., *Black Slave Narratives* (New York: Macmillan Co., 1970), pp. 192–194.

William Still's Account of Harriet Tubman, c. 1870: from William Still, *The Underground Railroad* (Chicago: Johnson Publishing Co., 1970), pp. 305–306.

Harriet Beecher Stowe, *Uncle Tom's Cabin; or, Life Among the Lowly,* 1852: excerpted in Andrist, *The American Heritage History,* p. 333.

The Last Chapter of *Uncle Tom's Cabin,* 1852: from King, *United States History,* p. 171.

Julia Lovejoy's Letter to a New Hampshire Newspaper, September 5, 1856: from "Selected Letters from Kansas, 1855 to 1863," in Ken Burns's *American Stories,* PBS.

Chief Justice Roger B. Taney's Opinion in *Dred Scott v. Sandford,* March 1857: from *The Annals of America,* vol. 8, 1850–1857 (Chicago: Encyclopaedia Britannica, 1980), pp. 440f.

Lincoln's "House Divided" Speech, 1858: from John Gabriel Hunt, ed., *Words of Our Nation* (New York: Gramercy Books, 1993), p. 82.

Stephen Douglas's Response to Lincoln, 1858: from Milton Meltzer, *Voices from the Civil War* (New York: Thomas Y. Crowell, 1989), p. 19.

A Telegraphed News Dispatch from Baltimore, October 17, 1859: from Horace Greeley, *The American Conflict,* 1864; excerpts in Andrist, *The American Heritage History,* p. 332.

John Brown's Prediction, December 2, 1859: from Meltzer, *Voices from the Civil War,* pp. 20–24.

William Russell, *My Diary, North and South,* 1863: from Meltzer, *Voices from the Civil War,* pp. 26–27.

Nathaniel Hawthorne's "Sketches," 1862: from Meltzer, *Voices from the Civil War,* pp. 27–30.

PART III   The War Begins

George Ticknor's Letter to an English Friend, April 21, 1861: from Henry Steele Commager, *The Blue and the Gray: The Story of the Civil War as Told by Participants* (New York: Fairfax Press, 1982), pp. 46–47.

Paul Burns's Letter to a Missouri Friend, June 1861: from Andrew Carroll, *War Letters: Extraordinary Correspondence from American Wars* (New York: Washington Square Press, 2001), p. 49.

Marietta (Ohio) *Home News Extra,* April 13, 1861: from *The Boisterous Sea,* p. 505.

The Memoirs of Captain Abner Doubleday, April 1861: from Abner Doubleday, *Reminiscences of Forts Sumter and Moultrie,* in Commager, *The Blue and the Gray,* p. 358.

Theodore Upson's Recollections, 1861: from Oscar O. Winthur, ed., *With Sherman to the Sea: The Civil War Letters, Diaries and Reminiscences of Theodore Upson* (Baton Rouge: Louisiana State University Press, 1943), pp. 38f.

Dr. Nott's Letter to a Friend, July 23, 1861: from Commager, *The Blue and the Gray,* p. 105.

The Account by William H. Russell, July 1861: from Cotner, *Readings,* pp. 345f.

PART IV   Stalemate East and West

The Recollections of Warren Lee Goss, 1890: from Warren Lee Goss, *Recollections of a Private: A Story of the Army of the Potomac* (New York: Crowell Publishing Co., 1890), in Meltzer, *Voices from the Civil War,* pp. 39–40.

The Memoirs of Major Abner R. Small, 1861: from Harold Adams Small, ed., *The Road to Richmond: The Civil War Memoirs of Major Abner R. Small* (Berkeley: University of California Press, 1957), excerpts in Meltzer, *Voices from the Civil War,* pp. 45–46.

The Recollections of Alexander Hunter, 1862: from Alexander Hunter, *Johnny Reb and Billy Yank* (New York: Neal Publishing Co., 1905), in Commager, *The Blue and the Gray,* pp. 742–744.

General McClellan's Dispatches to Washington, D.C., 1862: from James M. McPherson, *Battle Cry of Freedom: The Civil War Era* (New York: Ballantine Books, 1988), p. 525.

General Law's Account of Robert E. Lee, 1862: from Evander M. Law, "The Fight for Richmond," *Southern Bivouac* 2, April 1867, in Commager, *The Blue and the Gray,* pp. 126–128.

The Observations of Sallie Putnam, June 1862: from Sallie Putnam, *Richmond During the War: Four Years of Personal Observation by a Richmond Lady* (New York: G. W. Carleton, 1867), pp. 119–120, excerpted in Commager, *The Blue and the Gray,* pp. 124–125.

Robert L. Dabney, *The Life and Campaigns of Lt. General Thomas J. Jackson,* 1866 (New York: Blelock & Co., 1866), pp. 516–518, excerpted in Commager, *The Blue and the Gray,* p. 172.

New York Daily Tribune, 1885: from B. A. Botkin, ed., *A Civil War Treasury of Tales, Legends, and Folklore* (New York: Promontory Press, 1981), pp. 174–175.

Lawrence Van Alstyne's Diary, September 1862: from Lawrence Van Alstyne, *Diary of an Enlisted Man* (New Haven: Turtle, Morehouse & Taylor Co., 1910), pp. 29–31; reissued, New York State Historical Association, 1964, pp. 32–33.

"The Battle Hymn of the Republic," February 1862: adapted from Commager, *The Blue and the Gray,* pp. 572–573.

Rose O'Neal Greenhow's Diary, March 1862: from Rose O'Neal Greenhow, *My Imprisonment* (London, 1863); excerpted in Josef and Dorothy Berger, eds., *Diary of America* (New York: Simon & Schuster, 1957), pp. 426f.

New York Herald, August 1862: from J. Matthew Gallman, *The Civil War Chronicles* (New York: Crown Publishers, 2000), pp. 211–212.

Lincoln's Reply to Greeley, August 1862: from Emily Davie, ed., *Profile of America* (New York: Thomas Y. Crowell, 1957), p. 277.

Union Major Rufus Dawes's Memoirs, 1862: from General Rufus Dawes, *Service with the Sixth Wisconsin Volunteers* (Marietta, Ohio: E. R. Alderman & Sons, 1890), excerpted in Commager, *The Blue and the Gray,* p. 213.

General John B. Gordon, *Reminiscences of the Civil War* 1862 (New York: Charles Scribner's Sons, 1903), pp. 81f; excerpts in Commager, *The Blue and the Gray,* pp. 224–225.

Lincoln's Emancipation Proclamation, September 22, 1862: adapted from Hunt, *Words of Our Nation,* pp. 94–96.

Charlotte Forten's Diary, January 1863: from Brenda Stevenson, ed., *The Journals of Charlotte Forten Grimke* (New York: Oxford University Press, 1988); excerpted in Louis P. Masur, ed., *"The Real War Will Never Get in the Books": Selections from Writers during the Civil War* (New York: Oxford Universtiy Press, 1993), pp. 153f.

Lewis Douglass's Letter to His Fiancée, July 1863: from Milton Meltzer, ed., *In Their Own Words: A History of* the American Negro, 1619–1865 (New York: Thomas Y. Crowell, 1964), pp. 94–96.

PART V The Turning of the Tide

Confederate William Owens's Account, December 1862: from William M. Owens, "A Hot Day on Marye's Heights," in *Battles and Leaders of the Civil War* (New York: Century Company, 1888; reissued by Grey Castle Press, Lakeville, Conn., 1989), pp. 217–219.

The Memoirs of Union Major Frederick Hitchcock, December 13, 1862: from Gallman, *The Civil War Chronicles*, pp. 254–256.

The Memoirs of Brigadier General Frederick Dent Grant, 1863: from Willard Webb, *Crucial Moments of the Civil War* (New York: Bonanza Books, 1961), p. 149.

An Anonymous Account by a Confederate Soldier, May 1863: from Gallman, *Chronicles,* p. 306.

The Recollections of Augustus Buell, July 1, 1863: from "The Canoneer," *Recollections of Service in the Army of the Potomac* (Washington, D.C.: National Tribune, 1890), pp. 63f.; excerpted in Commager, *The Blue and the Gray,* pp. 603f.

General James Longstreet's Memoirs, July 1863: from Gallman, *Chronicles,* p. 326.

Arthur J. L. Freemantle, "The Battle of Gettysburg," July 1863: from *Blackwood's Edinburgh Magazine* 94 (1863); reprinted in Commager, *The Blue and the Gray,* pp. 636–638.

The Diary of Josiah Gorgas, July 28, 1863: from Frank E. Vandiver, ed., *The Civil War Diary of General Josiah Gorgas* (Birmingham: University of Alabama Press, 1947), p. 55; quoted in McPherson, *Battle Cry of Freedom,* p. 665.

William Lusk's Letter, July 7, 1863: from Commager, *The Blue and the Gray,* pp. 638–639.

Lincoln's Gettysburg Address, November 19, 1863: from Susan McIntire, ed., *The American Heritage Book of Great Speeches for Young People* (New York: John Wiley & Sons, 2000), p. 92.

The Diary of Louisa May Alcott, January 4, 1863: from Gallman, *Chronicles,* p. 273.

Clara Barton's War Diary, 1864: from William E. Barton, *The Life of Clara Barton, Founder of the American Red Cross* (Boston: Houghton Mifflin Co., 1922), vol. 1, pp. 277–279.

John L. Ransom's Diary, 1864: from John L. Ransom, *Andersonville Diary* (Auburn, N.Y.: 1881); excerpted in Berger, *Diary of America,* pp. 435, 438f.

PART VI The Fall of the Confederacy

From the Memoirs of Private Warren Goss, May 1864: from Warren Goss, *Recollections of a Private: A Story of the Army of the Potomac* (New York: Thomas Y. Crowell, 1890), pp. 268f.; excerpted in Commager, *The Blue and the Gray,* pp. 979f.

The Memoirs of Horace Porter, May 1864: from Horace Porter, *Campaigning with Grant* (New York: Century Publishing Co., 1897); excerpted in Robert Hendrickson, *The Road to Appomattox,* (New York: John Wiley & Sons, 1998), p. 28.

The Journal of Eliza Andrews, December 1864: from Eliza Frances Andrews, *The War-Time Journal of a Georgia Girl* (New York: D. Appleton Co., 1908), pp. 32–33; excerpted in King et al., *United States History* (Menlo Park, Ca: Addison-Wesley Publishing Co., 1986), pp. 301–302.

Sherman quote on "War is cruelty . . ." in Hendrickson, *Road to Appomattox,* pp. 98–99.

General Grant's Memoirs, April 9, 1865: from Davie, *Profile of America,* pp. 282f.

Mary Boykin Chesnut's Diary, April 19, 1865: from Isabella Martin and Myrta Lockett Avary, *Mary Boykin Chesnut: A Diary from Dixie* (New York: Appleton-Century-Crofts, 1905); excerpted in Berger, *Diary of America,* pp. 458f.

PART VII Restoring the Union

From Booker T. Washington's *Up from Slavery,* 1872: excerpted in Meltzer, *In Their Own Words,* pp. 46f.

Scribner's Monthly, August 1875: from King et al., *United States History,* p. 306.

INDEX